Poker Genius

Poker Genius

The Mind Secrets of the Champions

DR. STEPHEN SIMPSON

ISBN-13: 9781537449487
ISBN-10: 1537449486
Library of Congress Control Number: 2016914946
CreateSpace Independent Publishing Platform
North Charleston, South Carolina

Contents

Foreword by Chris Moorman

M Y JOURNEY WITH Stephen started in January 2014. I had heard of mind coaches, but to be honest, I was skeptical about how much help they could give to a player like me—or anyone else, for that matter. However, I had no doubts I wanted more success and was prepared to try anything to give me that extra edge.

Like many people, I believe the New Year is a time to reflect upon the past and dream of the future. I had a lot to be happy about back then: As a professional poker player, I was doing the job I loved, and I was definitely living the dream. What could be better than traveling to exotic locations and playing poker with my best friends? The problem was that 2013 had been my toughest time in poker.

Prior to the World Series of Poker (WSOP) in 2013, I had been forced to get out of backing because I had overextended myself and had made a lot of bad decisions along the way. My poker bankroll had taken a big hit, and I had been forced to drop down in stakes and concentrate predominantly on online poker until I was in a better situation. I decided that once I did get in a better place, I would allow myself the luxury of traveling the live circuit again. But this plan did not go as well as I had hoped. As I became more focused on how much I was winning rather than just playing every hand as optimally as I could, I found I quickly became overly negative. I didn't like the person I was becoming and decided the problem was serious enough that I would talk to someone about it—but who was the best person to reach out to?

A friend of mine suggested Stephen Simpson, a doctor and mind coach from the United Kingdom. He had been working with Liv Boeree, and whether it was coincidental or not, her form had been transformed. To cut a long story short, Stephen and I spoke on the phone a couple of times and agreed to meet. The problem was that both of our diaries were very full, and unless we met in February, the next opportunity would be several months away. So we met for the first time in Vancouver and discussed a ton of stuff I had never told anyone about before. In these sessions we did some basic meditation and breathing exercises, and I talked about what I wanted to achieve in life, both inside and outside of poker.

Stephen mentioned I needed to find the zone while playing, and if I could do that, then good things would happen for me. The key to finding the zone was to be solely focused on poker while playing, but it was equally important to work on myself as a person and consistently set goals.

I enjoyed these sessions with Stephen, and I'm sure they helped me see things in a different light. It is worth noting that I went on to win my first-ever major live tournament, the 2014 World Poker Tour L.A. Poker Classic, just two weeks after my first meeting with Stephen and topped a field of 534 players to pocket $1,015,000.

I've always been an extremely competitive person—which is key to being a professional poker player—but it can be a hindrance in this game. At times you want to win too much, which forces you into making mistakes. This happened to me in 2014 at the WSOP in Vegas. I felt like I had never been more ready to take home one of those shiny bracelets. Unfortunately, this approach completely backfired because I had been trying too hard to win the tournament on day one.

I was a big chip leader in the LAPC main event, with four people left, and felt so close to winning the title that, in between hands, I was already thinking about what to say in the winner's interview! That all quickly changed, though, because I became complacent, which led to my making a few mistakes in huge hands. On top of this, I didn't allow my mind to let those mistakes go, and I even ended up misreading my hand in a key spot. Fortunately, I went on break at the right time, remembered the important things Stephen had taught me, and just did a little mental reset. After the break, and with nothing left to lose, I was able to make a comeback and show that, no matter how bad your situation at the poker table is, you should never give up.

I recommend you read this book from cover to cover. It not only explains in simple terms what you need to do to find the zone but also (and more importantly) how to make your own luck. It is crammed with practical tips to take you there too. You will not need to use all of Stephen's tips, so just choose what feels right for you. Trust your own experience, which you've gained over thousands of hours of working on your game. You deserve your reward.

Perhaps we will meet one day on the final table. I certainly hope so!

Note: Chris, known online as Moorman1, is now considered the most accomplished online poker player of all time and became the first player ever to achieve the $13 million milestone in lifetime online tournament winnings on PocketFives. With an astounding twenty-five wins, Moorman was also recently ranked the number one online player in the world and all-time PocketFives Triple Crown leader.

Introduction

THIS BOOK IS a system of seven secrets based upon sound scientific, psychological, and philosophical principles that will help you become a poker genius. It is a book about luck, winning, and gaining the edge.

I am convinced that luck is not random, and just in case you think this is too good to be true, be assured that I am not alone in this belief. Professor Richard Wiseman, in his provocative book *The Luck Factor*, proved that success is not an accident, and there are some very logical reasons that explain why this is so.

Some of my principles are logical, and some less so, but they have all worked for my clients. So how exactly will my system help you to attract more luck into your life and become a better poker player? Because the exercises are simple. Because you will be learning the secrets of the best. Because I will be with you every step of the way. Because you will not proceed to the next chapter until you are satisfied that you have identified what will work for you at each step.

Moreover, at the end of every chapter, you will choose the three elements from that particular chapter that most strongly resonate with you and write them down. When you keep things simple, you will spot more opportunities and make cleaner decisions.

When you ask people what one quality they most desire, very often their answer is "more luck." Napoleon Bonaparte probably would have agreed with them. When asked what was the most important quality that he looked for in his generals, he replied simply that he wanted only lucky ones. I do not financially back poker players, but if I did, I would definitely look for lucky players. I do, however, coach poker players, and we spend a considerable amount of time talking about luck and how we can attract more of it into our lives.

I also explain the system of seven secrets to them, as I will with you. I did not invent these secrets; most of them have been around for centuries. My mission has been to adapt them for my clients and myself and then use them to our benefit. Poker legend Chris Moorman is one of my clients, and this is how our journey together began.

March 1 was an important date in ancient Rome: it was the start of the New Year and dedicated to Mars, the god of war. On this date in 2014, Chris Moorman was fighting his own war, and it was not going well. In fact, he was facing near-certain defeat.

By day five of the World Poker Tour L.A. Poker Classic, Moorman had been slowly but surely grinding his path to the final table. It could have ended much earlier when, late on day one, he had gone all in on a weak hand. Luckily for him, his opponent folded, and Chris won another huge pot with his very next hand to climb into the top ten. (We will talk a lot more about luck throughout this book.)

On day five, Chris was thinking he had a good hand, with a jack and 3, as his hole cards, a "flop" of community cards shared by the players that were queen, 7, and 5; a "turn" community card of 4; and then finally a "river" fifth community card of 6. That meant a straight of 3-4-5-6-7, a strong hand, and he bet on it heavily. He felt good, but then disaster struck. To his horror, at the showdown, Chris saw that his hole cards were not jack and 3, but jack and 2—not a winning hand but a huge hit. Making such a fundamental error devastated Chris, and at that point, he was staring defeat in the face. The only good news was that the break was coming soon, and it would be an opportunity to regroup, talk to his partner, Kate, and remind himself of the techniques we had worked on only days before.

So what techniques did he draw upon in his hour of need? As you read this book, you will discover many of them. How you will use them is a different question, with a different answer. They'll include techniques you've probably never dreamed about—techniques that might make your friends laugh. However, please keep in mind that he or she who laughs last laughs best.

So Who Am I, and What Do I Do?

I am Stephen Simpson, a medical doctor and fellow of the Royal Society of Medicine. I have worked exclusively as a mind coach for the last eight years. In a nutshell, my role as a mind coach is to help my clients become winners. I show them how to operate at their peak performance level, which is usually much higher than they imagine possible. We achieve this together by using my system of psychological and other techniques that can ignite the massive latent power of their unconscious minds.

I enjoy talking to players whenever I can, and the same issues surface time and time again. These issues include dealing with losing runs, maintaining concentration, staying confident when on a tilt. This is a temporary state of confusion or frustration, and is a serious barrier to avoiding attention leaks, controlling emotions, and learning how to trust intuition. I will show you how to find solutions for all these issues and many others too. By the time you finish this book, you will have many new ideas to incite your skills. Even in the unlikely event that you have only a few new ideas, do not worry; a little goes a long way in poker, where a wafer-thin advantage can translate into a lot of money.

Until I started working with top players, my knowledge of poker was extremely limited. In my early career, I worked as a doctor in the oil fields in Africa and spent many happy hours playing poker with my friends. I always felt very welcome at the table, and it was only recently that I discovered the main reason why: It was because I left most of my money with the other players. So my poker playing did not last very long. Little did I know that, many years later, it would become an important part of my life.

In 2012, while in Portugal, I met an Irish student named Rory Brown. We shared several things in common. He was interested in psychology, for instance, and was studying in Dublin for a master's degree in psychotherapy. Rory was also a talented golfer, and we enjoyed playing together several times. Once, while we were chatting at the bar, he mentioned he was a semiprofessional poker player and was able to successfully fund his studies with his winnings.

As a mind coach, I was fascinated and wanted to know more about the skills poker requires. At that time, most of my work involved helping tour golfers improve their game by working on their mind skills. It did not take me long to realize that the skills required in golf are very similar to the ones Rory described for poker.

We spent many more hours exchanging ideas and experimenting with different techniques. In March 2013, we began to work together in a more organized way. I am pleased to say Rory really progressed and has since been posting some great results. He works incredibly hard, never stops thinking about the game, and thoroughly deserves his successes. These include winning over $1 million and making multiple high-profile final tables. Despite his rise to poker stardom, Rory remains humble and grounded, and he is one of the most genuine people one could hope to meet.

He found inspiration from our working together, but I am always mindful that it was Rory who played his cards, not I. However, it is certainly true that this book can impact your life in a positive way. As long as you read it to the end, of course!

Later in 2013, Rory was playing in Amsterdam when, one evening, he talked to a talented female player named Liv Boeree. Liv was considering consulting with a mind coach in the United States, and so Rory suggested she might want to contact me. He gave her my card, which she kept for several months.

In December 2013, Liv called me and asked if we could meet. To make a long story short, we met several times over the following weeks. During this time, I traveled with her to tournaments in Edinburgh and Dublin and learned a lot more about the exciting world of poker.

Liv had contacted me because, by her exceptional standards, 2013 had been a lean year, with live-event earnings of only $51,000. Her form returned immediately when we started working together: She won $129,000 in January 2014 alone and also placed second in a major event in Edinburgh. Liv found our work together revolutionary for her game, and her fine form continues to date, the highlight being her superb performance in Barcelona in August 2015, when her third-place finish earned her $449,000.

After her Edinburgh success, Liv talked to a friend of the legendary poker player Chris Moorman. Chris's results were not going his way either, and after he had received my contact details and we had exchanged a few calls, Chris and I agreed to work together. We still do—and we never stop learning even more about this beautiful but often-frustrating game.

The immediate results of our work together were spectacular, as fellow poker player and journalist Lee Davy recounted in his December 23, 2014, PokerUpdate.com article "Mind, Body and Soul with Dr. Stephen Simpson":

> I have interviewed a lot of poker players, and invariably I am thrusting a camera into their face just after they have won something.
>
> My most common questions are: "What are you doing differently? Where did this string of results come from?"
>
> The generic response is: "It's just variance."
>
> But is it really just variance?
>
> When Chris Moorman finally got that 300lb Gorilla off his back by winning the World Poker Tour (WPT) LA Poker Classic, was it variance, or was it something else?
>
> I think it was something else.
>
> Three weeks prior to Moorman's victory, Dr. Stephen Simpson flew out to Vancouver, Canada, to start a series of sessions with the world's most successful online tournament player in the history of the game.
>
> Three weeks later, Moorman won a million dollars in that LA tournament.[1]

This long-overdue maiden victory in a live event made a huge difference for Chris. I did not realize it at the time, but this achievement would also make a huge change in my life.

The Beautiful Game of Poker

Poker certainly is a beautiful game and also an extremely popular one. I have been surprised by how many people talk to me about poker, how many people watch it on TV, and how many people dream of being a poker star too. Is the attraction the money, the exotic travel, or perhaps the fantasy of being a rebel?

For many players, poker is a recreational hobby that costs them little if any money to play. For others, poker is a part-time job they engage in online to supplement their income; hopefully, any losses can be covered by their day jobs, and any damage is done to the players' dented pride more than to their bank account balances. For a minority of players, poker is a full-time occupation that involves long hours and much travel, often seven days a week. Irrespective of where you fit on this spectrum, you owe it to yourself to give yourself the best chance of winning more than your share of hands and achieving all the fame and fortune that might follow—if you are very, very lucky.

Chris Moorman is a professional player, and—far from being rebellious—he has a background that is conventional enough. Still, from the age of eleven, there were hints of what was to come: It was then that he found bridge, for instance, and he was good enough to captain England. He was pretty good at pool too, so he captained his university team and won the national university championship. While at Essex university, he also discovered that playing poker was a lot more fun than studying economics—and much more profitable too.

Moorman was born in July 1985 and has already won millions at the tables and online. Indeed, he is the first player to have broken the $13 million barrier in online events. Yet it is abundantly clear that life as a professional poker player is a tough one: It involves long, unsocial hours, long losing runs, and lots of stress. So what is the attraction? Fame and fortune are the obvious attractions, as is the exotic travel while on tour with fun-loving friends.

What else drives players to this sport to the exclusion of most other activities? Could it be that they are obsessed with playing poker or even addicted to it? Moorman knows this could be true and offers some extremely valuable cautionary words: "Yes, poker can be very addictive, but you have to realize that it is just a game and not let it take over your life. If you are playing online, you can set weekly or daily deposit limits, and it is wise to practice good bankroll management so that you don't end up losing money you can't afford (to lose)." Please do not ignore this critical advice from Chris. It should guide you on every step throughout your poker career. If this is difficult, then seek help—the earlier the better.

As mentioned previously, poker player and journalist Lee Davy has interviewed me on several occasions. In another article, titled "The Stephen Simpson School of Making Your Own Luck in Poker," he related our conversation about the importance of luck:

> "There is an old saying that people make their own luck, and I believe that's true to a certain extent," said Dr. Simpson. "People who tend to have a great outlook on life tend to believe that they are luckier than the average person, and this is true when placed under the microscope of scientific study."
>
> Is Simpson saying that luck is controlled by the way the poker player feels?
>
> "It seems rather simplistic, but to a large degree, yes that's true. If you have a more positive outlook on life, have more friends, a strong network, see opportunities, and have the confidence to try things that take you out of your comfort zone—then yes you'll have the best chance of creating your own luck."
>
> And finally it all makes sense.
>
> Dr. Simpson is talking about the ingredients that formulate a streak of winning results known as a heater. Everyone in poker understands this word. It's a run of results that sees all the stars align producing a long winning streak.[2]

So is your heater switched on at the moment? If not, where is it hiding? In the following chapters, I will do my best to help you answer these questions.

I have discovered the beauty of poker too, and I play online poker for money and thoroughly enjoy it. I even find it relaxing. My dream is to play in a big live event, and I am inching closer to it every day. However, I fortunately have skills in other areas too. I use these skills in my role as a mind coach—my first love—and my clients include some of the world's elite poker players. They know the value of maximizing every possible edge, and that includes developing their mental game. So do as they do: develop your mind skills to give yourself the best chance at finding the elusive heater switch that Davy described.

Great Theories, but Do They Work in Real Life?

These theories certainly do work in real life. While researching for this book, I became increasingly fascinated by the illogical concepts and philosophies associated with luck. Some of these concepts have been around for centuries whereas others are more recent. I experimented with these techniques on my clients and myself.

I was shocked and, on occasion, frightened by some of the results, which defied logical explanation. Could I use these techniques myself? There was only one way to find out. I chose a new project to test my techniques on and selected a subject I knew little about.

Online gaming is one of the fastest growth industries and generates billions of dollars in revenue for the companies that feed this market. Some of their clients have profited too, while others have not been so lucky. In any case, it is now possible to bet on almost anything, including political election results and even TV talent shows, so I had many choices. Poker is a huge market, as is sports betting. I chose to focus on predicting sporting-event results, largely because it is a subject I follow with passion. All the same, I knew it would still be a stiff challenge to get lucky. Did I succeed and make any money?

My Experiments with Luck Were a Bit Too Successful for Some

The answer is yes; I did make some money—not a huge fortune, but enough to buy a new car and enough for three international companies to drastically limit my accounts. How did I do it?

This book will explain how, and this is a taste of what is to come:

- How do you switch on your heater and thereby bring life to your goals?
- How do you build confidence, even if this does not come naturally?
- How do you construct vivid visualizations that become self-fulfilling prophecies?
- How do you develop mindfulness and connect to the vast power of your unconscious mind?
- How do you use the interconnected techniques of hypnosis, HeartMath, and Havening?
- Why are some people lucky while others are not?
- How do you use synchronicity and coincidence to put luck on your side and discover that quantum physics, relativity, string theories, and the law of attraction may all be related, even if you do not understand a single word of physics?

How to Make Luck and Intuition Your Best Friends

The overarching conclusion I reached in writing this book was that luck is inextricably linked to intuition. There is so much we can do to improve our intuition. All the secrets of success I describe develop priceless intuition skills. If you could improve your intuition, what difference would this make to your game? Are you ready to start this journey now? Good, because your journey will start with an examination of your unconscious mind.

Think about this: Life was not always so tough, and it was much simpler when you were a baby. From the very first day, you were 99.99 percent ready for life. You needed parental support, but all your systems and organs were formed and functioning perfectly. You did not need to think about your insulin metabolism or your immune system because they were automatic; they were governed by your unconscious mind. You did not really have a conscious mind at that point, but you soon began to acquire one. That is when your problems started.

Although it was only small, your conscious mind soon felt it was the most important thing in your life and that it was the boss. It is not a coincidence, but that is when life also became more complicated. Is it possible to go back to the easy life, knowing what you know now? It certainly is.

By reading this book, you will connect to the vast power of your unconscious mind; you will start to learn to trust your instincts and heightened intuition and listen more attentively to your inner voice. Then you will learn how to switch on your heater and bring your goals to life. The truth is that this is the secret to achieving success the easy way rather than the hard way.

You will likely start to immediately reap some benefits from reading this book. Any one chapter can propel your life to the next level. Read all the chapters, practice the exercises, and then be surprised by your discovery of just how high you can fly.

Magnify Your Magic

This book is also about magic. More specifically, it is about the magic of your mind, the fact that you are using only a fraction of what you could be using to make your life a whole lot easier and the fact that you can learn to magnify magic and use it as you will.

Magic is a special, mysterious, or inexplicable quality, talent, or skill. It is a subject that delights all children by tantalizing their imaginations. Sadly, it is something most adults reject—or do they? Does some deep recess of your mind believe your childhood magic is still alive—or do you have a vague conviction that your universe is not quite as random as it sometimes might appear? I hope so.

So what else can you expect from this book's alchemy? You can expect that I will explain how luck and magic appear to be linked. While both can exist independently, their combination increases their potency many times over. So set your sights high. The enemy of the best is the good. In other words, if you accept the good, then you are far less likely to achieve the best possible outcome. The best possible outcome waiting for you is your delight in being able to tune in to the creative deeper areas of your mind and see things with a new clarity.

For perhaps the first time, you will experience being the driver of your life rather than the passenger. You will be in control, imposing your demands on life rather than accepting the demands life imposes on you.

Learn from the Best

Save yourself a lot of time and frustration and ask yourself this question: "What do successful players do differently than I do?" In the following chapters, we will ask this question many times. We will study successful people to learn from them. Their success is not an accident, and it is not just a result of luck either—although, intriguingly, many successful people believe they create their own luck.

The following pages are filled with practical examples for you to use. These are based on my diverse experiences and were painstakingly and sometimes painfully gleaned from the university of life. You can also adapt the conclusions of the great thinkers in history because their views are as valid now as when they were living.

This book is not only about successful people but also about ordinary people like you and me because when ordinary people steal from the best, the results can be extraordinary. This book is about people who have found success in different ways. Reassuringly, some common strands have stood the test of time. At least one of these might point you in the right direction when you feel a little lost in an increasingly confusing world; embrace two or more strands, and who knows where your journey might end.

How to Get the Most out of This System

How you use this book will determine, to a large extent, what you receive from it. It will take some commitment, but not as much as you might fear. Make the effort; it will be worth it.

Life would be simple if I could just let out all the secrets to success right now. You could then memorize and use them immediately. Indeed, I *could* share some secrets right away. I know that at least one of them would help you, and you would probably be very happy with it. I'm not going to, though, for two fundamental reasons: First, you would add me to your long list of all the well-intentioned people in your life who have tried to persuade you to do stuff "for your own good," and most people's lists are way too long already. Second, a much bigger prize is almost within your reach and certainly a lot closer than you can imagine.

The secrets are good. But the ideas that come from your own mind will be so much better; indeed, they will be the best ideas for you.

My role is only to tickle your brain. More specifically, it is to tickle the large bit of your brain that you are not using to anywhere near its full potential—your unconscious mind. Let me give you an example. In my work as a mind coach, it makes no difference to me whether my client is a sports star, business mogul, TV celebrity, or friend who lives next door. When I see a client for the first time, I ask for only two things: First, I want my client to have an open mind. I have no problem with skepticism; that is to be expected. Indeed, it is a healthy attitude as long as it is also combined with an open mind. Second, I require a note detailing the client's issue before our session. This note is vital to me for a number of reasons, not the least of which is because it describes the client's view of his or her problem at a superficial level and projects a desired outcome. Ultimately, my client will use this yardstick in measuring our success, or lack of it, while working together.

At a deeper level, something magical often happens when my clients write their notes to me; they take on a life of their own. I start to appreciate the words the clients use, I gain a glimpse of their view of the world and what makes them tick, and I start to develop the skeletons of strategies that I believe they will find helpful. Their notes are often anything but brief. The magic is often hidden in the final paragraph, and here's an example: "Steve, I'm sorry I rambled on a bit. I hadn't thought of some of these things for years. You will be really surprised, but I feel a lot better already, just for writing this down."

We have all probably heard something similar and so are not in the least surprised, because this is how the mind works. Writing about a problem often helps.

So I'd like to stress this fundamental point with you right now: writing is the doing part of thinking.

This sentence is really important, which is why it has appeared so early in this book. It is important because writing is one simple way to connect to the unconscious mind. It can put us into a flow state, like the zone in sports or the groove that musicians describe. These are creative places to be because these are places where many successful ideas germinate and grow. It is also a great place for your mind to be while playing poker.

The Magic of Thinking in Colors

So use this book for writing as well as reading—scribble to your heart's content. You may wish to use highlighters. Use your favorite color to mark whatever most strongly resonates with you; use a neutral color for everything you are not sure about. In time, you will cross some of these out. Other bits will turn to your favorite color right in front of you. Whatever is left may take a long time to digest and can be safely ignored for the moment.

At the end of each chapter, you will find a section called "In a Nutshell." Briefly review the chapter, your scribbled notes, and your highlighted text. Identify three points you believe can help you to immediately (or at least in the very near future) ignite your poker skills, and then write them down at the end of each chapter. These are what I call nuggets, and in the right circumstances, they can be worth their weight in gold.

Spend a few minutes thinking about how you could use these three points in some part of your life. Make a commitment to discuss these points with your friends and others you trust, just as you probably already share your poker-hand histories. These are all great ways to feed ideas into your unconscious mind so that it can digest them at its leisure.

I'll put it another way:

- Well-intentioned thoughts often remain just as thoughts.
- Spoken thoughts sometimes get done.

- Written thoughts often lead to unimagined success.
- Shared thoughts ignite skills that you did not know you possessed.

Let me share a word of warning here. All successful coaches know that as their clients become excited by new ideas, their confidence grows and results improve. They also know that a month later, these clients are often back where they started, because change is difficult to cement, and it is all too easy to slip back into the comfort zone. Do not let this be you. I will explain how to avoid this common trap in the final chapter.

In the rest of this book, I will describe what I believe to be the seven most important mind secrets that can form the solid foundation for all other strengths you will require to be a complete champion. These other strengths include long hours of deep practice, an understanding of mathematics and statistics, resilience, and the driving belief in self and ability to withstand the heat of battle.

What if you don't play poker and are reading this book because of idle curiosity—or perhaps for some other reason? Guess what? These mind secrets work pretty well in all other areas of life too.

These Are the Results You Can Expect

I wish I could guarantee that these mind secrets will make you a winner. Unfortunately, I cannot. However, I can guarantee that they will make you a much stronger player than you are right now and a player more able to cope with the capricious demands of Lady Luck. They will also make you a happier player. Without question, this is the most important point, because happy players are good players. When the fun stops, then so should you. Definitely.

At the end of this book, I will suggest how to use the action points you will have developed from the few nuggets that most strongly resonated with you in each chapter.

Now, you are almost ready to get started. Fasten your seat belt, and step on the gas. Do you know where you are going? Can you be sure the map you are holding is accurate? Can you trust it? No, no, and no. But this is a time for courage—a time to go forth bravely, as somebody once said, to confront reality.

For what it's worth, most people are not sure what constitutes reality. "Reality is merely an illusion, albeit a very persistent one," said Albert Einstein, so apparently he was just as unsure about reality as we are now. This uncertainty complicates our mission more than a little. But at a deeper level, it also makes it a lot easier, because it will help us destroy the barriers that surround us and release the power of our imaginations where there are no limits. In the following chapters, we will frequently return to Einstein's sage words, one way or another.

As you travel more deeply into this book, do not be surprised if you turn the pages faster and faster. Some have read it cover to cover in a single sitting. Others limit themselves to a chapter a day and look forward to it as a break from the table or the screen. Go with your instincts, but be sure to spend some time pondering as well. Then you cannot fail to become a better player.

Now, review your notes and thoughts on this chapter. Ask yourself this question: "What three things can I do now that can help me immediately, or at least in the very near future, to make more luck playing poker?" Write your three points below.

In the next chapter, I will share my thoughts about why so many people do not really know what they want from life. Realizing something is missing but not knowing what it is makes people feel frustrated. I will also reveal how surprised Chris Moorman was the first time we met, when I suggested he should stop playing poker for money!

In a Nutshell—Three Nuggets

1.

2.

3.

1

How to Achieve Your Goals

THE FOLLOWING IS a true story and deserves your careful consideration. This will not turn on your heater, but as your reward, it will plug you into the electrical socket and serve as a vital first step toward seeing the money.

I was sitting in my hotel room in Vancouver in February 2014. Sitting opposite me was Chris Moorman, fixing me with a steely gaze. I knew then what a lamb feels like in the slaughterhouse and why Chris is one of the most feared poker players in the world. I had just flown halfway across the world and checked into a luxury hotel to meet Chris for the first time. It had been my decision, and I had broken all my rules. No agreement, no contract, and no upfront payments—a decision made on the spur of the moment. Was I crazy?

Chris clearly thought I was. "You can't be serious! Are you out of your mind?"

Actually, he remained silent, but I could guess what was going on in his mind. So I was on a bit of a tilt here, to say the least. I had just broken another one of my golden rules, not for the first time, and was all in on a hunch. In other words the time and money I had invested in this trip could be completely lost within the next few seconds.

This is how it happened. We had just started our first session of work together, and as usual with a new client, I had asked him what his goals

— 1 —

were. This was a pretty standard opening gambit. The problem started when he told me that his goals were to win his first live poker event and also earn more money. The reason I had a problem was that I had just suggested to Chris that these goals would not be very helpful. I dug myself even deeper into the pit when I suggested we would never talk about things like this again. Looking at Chris's face, I did not need to be Mystic Meg to predict that he was ready to head out the door.

I had only one chance left. I knew Chris was a passionate soccer fan, so I shifted our conversation to safer ground. I can't remember our exact words, but our conversation went something like this:

"It's a bit like taking a penalty kick in soccer" I explained.

"For a professional player, it should be just about the easiest part of the game," I continued. "Usually it is, but not if you are wearing an England shirt. Especially if you know that if you miss this crucial penalty kick, you and your team are out of the World Cup. Your mind can read the headlines in the newspapers back home. The fans are not going to be happy with you, and that is putting it mildly."

I had his attention now and went on.

"If I was coach for England I would tell my players to ignore the goalkeeper."

Gulp. A quick glance told me I was losing Chris again, so I hastily added these words: "The goals that I like and recommend are those that are within your control. The soccer player has no control over which way the goalkeeper will move once the kick has been made and whether the keeper will save the ball or not.

"The goal that I would recommend is that a player pick the smallest possible target and kick the ball in that direction, preferably hard. This is something the players practice all the time and do not need to think about. If their focus is entirely on their target, they have then suddenly increased their chances of success exponentially."

Chris leaned forward a little. I was already all in and had nothing more to lose. No pressure.

"So let me ask you a question," I said. "When you are sitting at the final table, what *can* you control?"

Chris's eyes flipped to the right. Usually this is a sign that a person is connecting with his or her imagination.

"I guess, when you put it like that, there's not much that I can control," he answered. "However, I can easily think of many things that are outside my control."

That was a great answer, so then it was time for my final question.

"Now, think of just one thing that you can control throughout the tournament and, indeed, in every game of poker you ever play in the future. One thought that will give you the best possible chance of winning."

This time his answer came back far more quickly.

"I guess I can commit to giving each card my total focus throughout the tournament. This will keep me grounded and ensure my mind is not distracted by other stuff going on."

This was exactly what I had hoped he would say. We spent the next three days working on his answer. Chris was the perfect student: He showed up on time, asked great questions, and did his homework. He scored particularly highly on his last computerized assessment, so as I left for the airport, I knew his head was in the right place and that the results would likely follow.

However, in my wildest imagination, I never expected he would win his first live event only days later.

Throughout the rest of this book, I will explain what I believe to be the seven secrets of peak performance—and of getting lucky. Some of these secrets I shared with Chris in Vancouver, but others I have developed and shared with him since then.

The first secret is to have the best possible goal in life, whether you are a poker player, a parent, a business executive, or anything else. Now, let me explain in more detail why I believe this is so important, how you can use this secret to your advantage, and what the best possible goal might be.

Do you ever feel that your life is missing something crucial, but you can't put your finger exactly on what it is? Like an irritating itch that won't go away? You look enviously at others, as they appear to achieve so much more with a lot less effort. You wonder, "What are they doing that I'm not?" And you try to discern why the good things you want in your life are so elusive.

These are the types of questions many people ask about their goals:

- Will I ever win a major live poker tournament?
- Will I ever meet my perfect partner?
- Will I ever earn enough money to pay my rent?

Most of these questions will probably be very familiar to you. The problem is that no matter how often you ask yourself these questions, the answers will not change. Worse, just asking these questions will add to your frustration. They will drain your precious energy and thoughts that could be used far more productively elsewhere in your life.

I will give you the same suggestion that I gave to Chris: It is time for you to stop asking these questions, lose your frustration, and discover how to make things happen for you the easy way. I will explain what I mean by this in a moment. But first, let me shake your foundation a little.

From an early age, you were likely told that the harder you work, the more successful you will be. The sooner you can throw away this well-intentioned but mistaken advice, the sooner you will start to live the life you deserve. While there is some truth in this statement, it is very far from being the whole truth. Because the whole truth is that countless examples exist to demonstrate how the more you strive for success, the more elusive it becomes.

Much more important is taking one moment at a time to stay in the present. The result is peak performance, also known as being in the zone or flow. This is what this book is about—how to attract more of what you want, with a lot less stress; not be dragged back by the past or worry about the future; and just stay in the present so that you recognize the opportunities that surround you. Unfortunately, society is far more con-cerned with big lofty goals than with the more important subject of our mundane day-to-day activities. This is a disastrous error, because how we choose to spend each minute of each day is one of the few things in life that we can control. Such moments form the building blocks that can shape our futures and our successes. Valuing these moments allows us to stay in the present.

The truth is that the more you measure things—especially results—the more elusive they become. I am not for a moment saying that results are not important. They are, but not when considered in isolation. Far more important are the small steps that you can control and that you take every day.

Focus on process, and the results will follow.

Rory Brown, who knows this better than most, said:

In highly competitive sports, business, and poker, where the prizes for winning are so handsome, it is hard not to be seduced by results-based thinking. If you win, you made the right decision; if you lose, you did something wrong.

With poker, the element of luck or variance is so obvious that it's hard to wrap one's head around it. Often you will be rewarded for making the wrong decision; likewise, and much more scarring to our psyche, you will be punished for making the correct decision.[3]

"Scarring to our psyche?" Wow! Perhaps by now you are beginning to realize how important mind skills and this book will be to your development as a competent and well-rounded poker player.

Self-Knowledge

The good news is all people have something amazing inside them, and this includes you, for certain. All you need to do is find where it is hiding, and then you will start building that edge to use against the other players at the table. Most of them do not know this stuff, or they discount it as too fanciful.

Not Aristotle, though, because he knew a thing or two about what makes us tick. He explained a long time ago, "Knowing yourself is the beginning of all wisdom."

Not much has changed over the last twenty-three hundred years. When the same message about the importance of self-knowledge keeps surfacing repeatedly over the centuries, we can be fairly sure of its enduring value. The reason self-knowledge is so important is that with it we can plan our lives and develop authentic goals to structure order from chaos, thereby increasing our own luck. Lucky poker players know who they are, what they want, and how to achieve their goals. These are some of the reasons why they are lucky and why you can be too.

Without self-knowledge, we drift or, even worse, waste our time and energy on meaningless goals or ones beyond our control. The truth is that most of us struggle with developing and sustaining a sense of purpose; many of our ancestors did too. This is why this chapter is so important and is the logical starting point of our journey.

Some of the following chapters will also describe relatively simple techniques that can improve your knowledge of yourself. So as you read this book, do not be surprised if your goals change. This may feel a little confusing, but do not worry—all will be revealed in the final chapter. But please do not read it now! There are a few other things to learn first.

Choose a Wonderful Goal to Ignite Your Genius

The secret to achieving any goal is to make sure it is the right one for you. You will certainly have plenty of advice from others, but I suggest you ignore them. This is all about you, your poker, and whatever else is most important to you in your life. The right sort of goal is, therefore, critical. If you do not know where you are going, then any road will take you there, but it will be a long journey, and it may not be a happy one. Taking the shortest route relates to choosing the correct goal.

Ideally, you should have one overarching goal in life. I suggest you take some time before deciding what this might be. It is very easy to think of an impressive goal. But is it the right one? Is it something you want to achieve, or is it something your parents, teachers, or friends have recommended? Is it a goal that society regards as worthy rather than something you have always wanted to do?

For most of your life—at school, at work, and at home—you have been conditioned, to a certain extent, to recognize success by the monetary value of your possessions. Society places less value on qualities that cannot be measured so easily and yet are far more important.

There is nothing wrong with material goals. In this affluent world, most of us dream of having big houses, great cars, and fat bank account balances but forget those who cannot even dream of eating their next meal. So make your goal the means to an end and the result of doing other things skillfully along the way. When you reach your goal, do not be surprised when you look back and realize that the real fun was in the journey, not the destination.

In his book *Awaken the Giant Within*, Tony Robbins makes a powerful point that is well worth careful thought: "Achieving goals by themselves will never make us happy in the long term; it's who you become, as you overcome the obstacles necessary to achieve your goals, that can give you the deepest and most long-lasting sense of fulfillment."[4] Many mountaineers describe a sensation of anticlimax after a particularly difficult climb. They remember the journey that took them there with much more lasting satisfaction. Athletes who have trained for years to win an Olympic gold medal enjoy a temporary euphoria that is often replaced by a vague sadness or even depression. Their goal was their life. So what is left when they have achieved their goal?

Certainly dream of that big house and enjoy it when you own it; however, do not be surprised if, once you own your new house, your goal has changed its shape to a greater or lesser extent. If your goal was to own an even bigger house, then many more house moves may be in store for you. If you have a new goal that germinated during your journey, then perhaps you stumbled across some unexpected open doors. This is what people call serendipity, coincidence, synchronicity, or just a healthy dose of luck. We will talk much more about these compelling mysteries in later chapters.

Here is another thought from motivational guru Tony Robbins. He gives a stark and somewhat nihilistic message on the dangers that haunt the unwary: "You will become by and large what your friends expect you to become." This might feel like the easier path—to conform to others' expectations of you. But we know on the inside when something is missing. In time, this feeling builds into dissatisfaction and even stress. Nothing clouds your judgment and performance more certainly than stress, especially if it is prolonged. So stress is the last thing you need when playing poker.

When people follow their passion, they are rarely disappointed. At present, how do you spend your money after paying all the bills? How do you spend your free time? What activity makes time fly; fills you with deep contentment either during or after; and in a humble and grounded way, lets you know this is something you are rather good at?

How many of your answers to these questions concern poker? In other words, how important is poker to you right now, and for what reasons?

If you are still struggling to identify what makes you happy and how you would like to spend the rest of your life, then you might like to try a simple exercise.

I hope you are happy and healthy right now. That said, while I normally encourage only positive thoughts, there is always an exception to every rule. This is it: Spend a few moments imagining how you would feel if you had just been told you had only six more months to live. How would you use this time? What would you do differently? What would each day look and feel like? Would you still play poker?

Now, readjust your thoughts back to your present situation. Are any of the changes you considered just a few moments ago still appropriate? If so, what would it take to make them possible? After you read this book, you will have a clearer picture of what you want, more ideas on how to achieve it, and the tools to make it easier than you dreamed. You lucky person!

How to Live the Dream

Once you have decided on your goal, the more you remind yourself of it each day, the more successful you are likely to be. The many ways to do this include writing the goal on sticky notes and sticking them on the bathroom mirror and the refrigerator or using the goal as the screen-saver on your computer, mobile phone, and alarm clock. The more places you can think of to display your notes, the more likely you are to reach your goal. It directs your unconscious mind and helps build a self-fulfilling prophecy. Keep in mind that writing is the doing part of thinking and a powerful connection to your unconscious mind. As President Abraham Lincoln said, "A goal properly set is halfway reached."[5]

Olympic swimming champion Michael Phelps said, "People say that I have great talent, but in my opinion, excellence has nothing to do with talent. It is about what you choose to believe and how determined you are to get there."[6]

He also said, "The mind is more powerful than anything else."[7]

It certainly is more powerful than anything else, yet so few people really believe this. Champions know this is true, and so each chapter in this book will provide opportunities for you to explore your own mind in new ways; open doors to your mind that you never knew existed; and open doors to more luck, health, wealth, and happiness than you thought possible. How many truths do we not see because our minds are elsewhere? How much of our precious time have we wasted searching for something that cannot be found but only perceived through intuition?

Our brains love questions, and the response is always more creative than when we just follow orders. However, we have enjoyed enough puzzles for the moment.

Now, review your notes and thoughts on this chapter. Ask yourself this question: "What three things can I do now that can help me immediately, or at least in the very near future, to make more luck playing poker?" Write your three points below.

In the next chapter, we will continue our journey and examine the importance of confidence to our success. We will discover how the power of our thoughts can create a massive and positive effect on our confidence. One thing is for sure: Poker requires huge player confidence. Chris Moorman has written much about confidence, and he has plenty of it. But a little more of it often helps a lot more than we might expect.

In a Nutshell—Three Nuggets

1.

2.

3.

2

Inner Confidence

CONFIDENCE IS A very influential component of getting lucky and playing great poker and is therefore also the second secret. It should come as no surprise that lucky people and great poker players have a huge amount of confidence. What may surprise you is that I can guarantee to significantly increase your confidence levels; all you have to do is meet me halfway by practicing the techniques in this chapter.

The challenge to overcome is that confidence is a fragile flower for all of us. Chris Moorman openly admitted that, in the space of a sixty-minute level, he practically destroyed his chances of winning his first live event. He was on a tilt, and his confidence in his game was at an all-time low. Fortunately, when we had worked together, we had planned for all kinds of different scenarios, including this one. So luckily, the next break came at just the right time for Chris to remember some of the things we had talked about and regroup.

My definition of confidence describes a quality other people have more of than we do. We look enviously at them and wish we could be more confident too. The truth is that we can be. In this chapter, I will describe several simple techniques you can practice to attract more confidence into your life—and curiously, luck often follows confidence.

You have to look at yourself every day, and what you see in the mirror will dictate to a large extent what you feel about yourself, good or bad, for the rest of the day. It will determine how confident you feel. You may judge your physical appearance or assess your personality or what you have achieved (or more likely not achieved) in your life, but this is not a helpful strategy.

William Shakespeare probably did not play poker, but if he had, I would have backed him. Consider this powerful message from his play *Measure for Measure*, and in times of doubt, recall his words and be brave:

Our doubts are traitors

And make us lose the good we oft might win

By fearing to attempt.[8]

The last thing we need when sitting at the poker table is to have traitorous doubts. These doubts will make it much more difficult to find the intuitive mind-set required to play our best. So how can we banish them or, at least, reduce their malign influence? We can start by cleaning up the voice in our head, known as our internal dialogue.

I Hear Voices in My Head. Am I Going Crazy?

No, you are not going crazy, because each person has at least one voice in his or her head. This voice is often a constant commentary of your life, and more often than not, it is not flattering. Very often the words slip out of our mouths, usually followed by an embarrassed "I was just talking to myself."

The problem is that this voice controls our thoughts, and our thoughts control our moods, so what goes on in our heads will surface in our lives sooner rather than later. Henry Ford expressed this succinctly when he said, "Whether you think you can or think you can't—you are right."[9] In other words, if you think you are not in the mood to play poker today, then chances are you will not be surprised by your poor results. Fortunately, the opposite is also true. Develop a positive attitude, value your talents, and approach challenges in this light, and your chances of success will increase significantly. So will your confidence level.

This first tip will demonstrate how you can build more confidence by cleaning up the voice in your head. Adopt the following simple mantra right now, and say it out loud: *"From this moment forward, I will say only good things about myself."*

If you are concerned that you might lose out on learning from your mistakes or that you are becoming arrogant, then you can add the following words: "Fear not. I can trust family, friends, and the rest of the world to point out my mistakes. I do not need to give them any help."

Remember the Good Times

There are other ways to increase your confidence and self-esteem. As with most things in life, they will require some preparation and effort on your part. However, considering the size of the glittering prize, they will be some of the best investments you will ever make. A powerful starting point is to make this commitment. Write it down; that way, you are much more likely to stick with it. Say it aloud and with conviction: *"From this moment forward, I will remember every good thing that happens to me."*

The reason this is so important is that most people remember all the things that have gone wrong in their lives but struggle to think of the many things that went right.

Practice makes perfect. Before you go to sleep at night, think of five things that went well during the day, and repeat this exercise when you wake up in the morning. Set yourself up for a great day at the table.

When somebody says something complimentary to you, or when something goes well for you, revel in the simple pleasure for a second or two longer than you ordinarily would before allowing that memory to slip into your unconscious mind. If you can do this several times a day for a month, then you will perceive a subtle change in your brain chemistry and outlook on life. You will notice the difference, but those closest to you will notice it more. You can enhance this effect by giving your brain another push in the right direction: When you have one of these pleasurable experiences, make sure the memory is easier to retrieve by associating it with a physical anchor. This is the memory equivalent of underlining or highlighting a statement in an article.

Some people press their thumb and forefinger together to reinforce a happy memory. Others touch their ear or brush their pants. Spend some time choosing your anchor. It should be discreet, but most importantly, it should feel right.

Adopt this practice for a month, and chances are you will continue to employ it in the future. These anchors will become seamless and automatic parts of your life.

Once you have mastered this technique, you will be ready for an advanced anchoring technique. This can be very powerful, but best results require you to be in a relaxed mental state.

So think of a time when you deeply experienced a flow state. Whatever it was that you were doing, it felt very easy, natural, and relaxed. At that time, you felt you could do no wrong. You probably wished you could bottle that special feeling, take it away, and then reproduce it in the future whenever you needed it most. The following technique does not require a bottle, but it can help you to enter your flow state a lot more easily and quickly than you ordinarily do.

Take your thoughts back to this special occasion and use your memory to add some detail to the picture in your mind. Where were you? What was the date? Who were you with? What clothes were you wearing? Do you remember any of your conversations with others? What other details can you add to this event?

When you are ready, take your time and answer this question: in only one word, how would you describe your feeling on this special day? Then answer this next question: if the special word had a color, what would it be?

Now we come to the most important question: how can you use this word and color to remind yourself of this special day, when you were experiencing flow, so that when you need to reproduce the same mental state in the future, you will be able to do so just as easily as you did today?

Jot down a few ideas now. Do not worry if they are not perfect, because in the next chapter, I will give you a few additional ideas to ponder.

Look Like You Feel and Feel Like You Look

There are many other powerful tools to enrich confidence. As another example, think for a moment of a person who is nervous or how you might look and feel when worried. Nervous people tremble, adopt withdrawn postures, and keep their heads held down. Their eyes and the rest of their bodies shift quickly.

This arousal is due to the physiological changes associated with the overstimulation of the autonomic sympathetic nervous system and the resultant effects of adrenalin and other hormones. It is known as the fight-or-flight response. If we hooked this person up to a biological monitor, then we would record many other physiological changes, including an increased heart rate, increased breathing rate, increased blood pressure, sweaty palms, and a dry mouth.

These changes prepare the body for instant action and are therefore, in the short term, valuable. In our modern society, however, much of our stress is due to emotional factors rather than causes that require immediate physical effort. The result is that we do not burn off the adrenaline and other hormones and so live in a constant state of stress and arousal. The medical consequences may be dire and include higher risks of hypertension, heart problems, anxiety, depression, and even cancer. The personal consequences are equally serious. You will find it difficult, if not impossible, to connect to your unconscious mind. As a result, your intuition will suffer, and this will not help your poker skills.

Stress is a killer. It takes life, it spoils life, and it gets in the way of attracting luck into your life. The good news is that there are several ways to eliminate stress or at least control it.

The autonomic nervous system was once thought to be beyond our conscious control. Now there is clear evidence that a degree of control is possible. This provides opportunities for us to overcome some of the dangerous effects of stress. For instance, Olympic archers and pistol and rifle athletes have learned how to control their heart rates to maintain a steady aim. Perhaps billiards and darts players have too, as have many top golfers. How many poker players have mastered these skills? Not many, and this can be a huge edge for you.

I spend some time every day making my edge, and this is one example of the benefits I have gained. I recently underwent cataract eye surgery and wanted only a local anesthetic because of a previous bad experience. Prior to the operation, I was able to drop my resting pulse rate to twenty-eight beats per minute. This provoked the alarm of the anesthetist until I explained that I was using deep meditation techniques. In later chapters, we will examine some of these methods in more detail

Another simple technique you can execute right now is to adopt a confident posture—the opposite of the previously described nervous posture.

Stand or sit tall, breathe deeply and slowly, move calmly, and smile. If you look confident, it will help you to feel confident.

Smiling is particularly important. If you don't believe me, then put a pencil between your teeth. This stretches the same muscles that you use when smiling, and so the pencil between your lips will make you feel a little bit happier.

These are examples of how the mind can affect our physiology, and the opposite is equally true. The mind and body are seamlessly linked, and by using these techniques, we can learn to use this fact to our advantage.

How is your posture at the table or when you play online at home? Probably not as good as it could be. So spend a little time practicing a confident posture, and then be prepared to feel differently and see surprising results.

Throughout the rest of this book, we will explore many more mental strategies that will allow you to overcome and eventually master these natural physiological responses. Such strategies involve the roles of breathing, meditation, mindfulness, hypnosis, and visualization as well as other ways to help you stay in the present.

Now, review your notes and thoughts on this chapter. Ask yourself this question: "What three things can I do now that can help me immediately, or at least in the very near future, to make more luck playing poker?" Write your three points below.

In the next chapter, we will continue our journey and examine the importance of visualization. We will discover how the power of our thoughts can create a self-fulfilling prophecy of success.

In a Nutshell—Three Nuggets

1.

2.

3.

3

Everyone Can Visualize

LUCKY PEOPLE AND successful people share one very important character-istic: They have very clear pictures in their heads of what they want to achieve. This is sometimes known as visualization and is the third of seven secrets to getting lucky.

Most of my professional poker clients have almost total certainty about their commitment to poker. They may have doubts about their ability and whether they have all the skill sets they need, but this is normal and why they ask for my help. And even so, they rarely doubt their love of poker, except during the most prolonged of tilts.

The seven secrets are not really separate subjects; they share many characteristics and build upon one another. In fact, visualization binds the first two secrets (goals and confidence) together and strengthens them.

So do not be concerned if you had difficulty identifying your goals. By the time you read this chapter and reflect internally on the bits that most strongly resonate, you will certainly have a much clearer picture in your mind of what you want and how you are going to get it. It might be related to poker, but it could be something entirely different. Just keep your mind open to possibilities, and sooner or later you will find the visu-alization that suits you best.

A vivid picture is a descriptive shortcut that takes fewer nerve cells to process than a verbal narrative—hence the expression "a picture is worth a thousand words." This picture is both a goal and a focus of concentration. Very often, what you see is what you get, so make sure to picture something you really want and not something you are trying to avoid. The brain often does not hear *no* or *not*, which can sometimes lead to terrible results.

The world of sports is full of examples: a poker player focusing on *not* losing a hand, a sprinter focusing on *not* starting before the gun is fired, a basketball player focusing on *not* missing this foul shot, etc. Guess what happens next?

Focusing on what you want to happen rather than on what you do not want to happen is as important in your business and personal life as it is when playing poker.

Some people are naturally very good at visualizing exactly what their body or mind is doing and what they want it to do. The good news is that these visualization skills can be taught and are available for everybody.

Muhammad Ali, perhaps the greatest boxer of all time, developed powerful visualization skills. One of my colleagues met him and asked about the secret to his success. He sighed wearily and explained, for the thousandth time, "I float like a butterfly and sting like a bee." My friend understood the sting, but he was still confused by the butterfly simile. Ali leaned closer and whispered, "I imagine floating out of my body, like a butterfly." He imagined he was standing at each corner of the ring and watching the fight from above. When he saw a muscle ripple in the shoulder of his opponent, he knew what type of punch was coming his way and had more time to avoid it.

Great scientists, especially those who work with abstract concepts, also have highly developed visualization skills. Albert Einstein is a famous example because he had magical visualizations. He explained that most of his creative thoughts were in pictures and that he rarely thought in words. This is another proof that a picture, or visualization, is worth a thousand words.

Time to Chill

These days, athletes are spending more time daydreaming with their eyes closed and less time in the gym or on the sports field. They are not lazy; nor are they wasting their time.

What they are indulging in is deep mental practice, and you should do the same.

The following experiment describes how competitive skiers prepared for a downhill run. Physiologists wired the skiers' muscles and attached them to recording machines in a scientific process called electromyography. They discovered that when skiers in the laboratory stand with their eyes closed and visualize their next competitive run, they all flex the same muscle groups at the same time, just as they would on the real run to mirror the ski terrain. This is called covert practice, described by Dr. Simon Jenkins, principal lecturer in sports coaching, as "covert (rather than overt) practice of a skill in that no actual movement occurs. It involves the use of imagery and verbal thoughts."[10]

Jenkins confirmed the value of mental practice too, from a scientific standpoint: "There is evidence to suggest that mental practice is better than no practice, and that mental practice in combination with physical practice is even better."

Develop visualizations of how you would like others to see you. Examples include visualizations of yourself sitting at your computer, entering a tournament hall, and sitting at the poker table. These will show you displaying the physical and emotional postures and mind-sets that you wish to project to others.

Now, you are ready to practice your own visualization of success and join the lucky people.

Go Large with Your Movie

Great movie directors know the importance of creating vivid imagery that engages all five of our senses—sight, hearing, touch, taste, and smell. These senses are our only information channels from our environments—environments that are limitless in their diversity. Everything is channeled through these conduits.

Now, it is time for you to direct your own movie. Make sure it is packed with detail relating to your five senses.

Let us get the cameras rolling. Lie back, close your eyes, and imagine some success you desire in the future, perhaps a few months from now. Imagine something you really want. Perhaps a big poker tournament is looming. Picture yourself achieving this success in as much detail as possible, using all your five senses.

What do you see? What do you hear? What do you feel, and where do you feel it? What do you taste and smell?

Reflect on all the things that you went through during the preceding few months to position you for this success. You will recognize that your processes were sound and that your journey was a series of small steps, not all of which seemed to be in the correct direction at the time.

Your thoughts are interrupted as a journalist from the local radio station approaches you and asks for the secret to your amazing success. Could you pass on some tips that would interest and help the station's listeners?

Pause to think for a few seconds, and then share some of the most illuminating insights and suggestions that you found most useful in achieving your wonderful result.

Most people like being asked to help others, and this is another reason why this simple visualization can be so powerful. What you have done is change your perspective: You have permitted your mind to create a vivid movie of a positive outcome in the future. You have also become the observer and watched yourself behave with unconscious excellence in this movie. Whenever you consciously change your perspective, you will profit by seeing yourself with greater clarity and more like others see you.

Sometimes there is danger in perceiving future goals as very remote, which may discourage you from even starting your journey. When projects are broken down into small steps, however, the most impossible task suddenly seems much more reachable.

Call on Your Virtual Friend

The following final visualization exercise brings together many of the concepts I have already described.

You have spent time choosing your goals wisely. You know about all the skills that will be necessary to reach your goal. You have practiced your confidence techniques, but you are still not certain that your ability is equal to the task. Not surprisingly, this negative thought decreases your chance of being successful.

So guide your mind in a different direction, and ask yourself this question: "Whom do I know who has all the skills I will need?" You do not need to know this person directly. It could be a famous poker player, scientist, or sports personality.

As this is a book about poker, you could do far worse than choose Chris Moorman as your role model, but there are plenty of other players to choose from. If you are female, how about choosing Liv Boeree? I have had the pleasure of working with Liv too, and she is an incredible person. I can also reveal that she has the most amazing visualization skills, and so it is no surprise that she is so successful.

Now it is your turn. Close your eyes, and imagine someone introduces you to this role model. He or she is happy to talk to you, and you have all the time in the world to ask your questions and listen to his or her advice.

Now, stretch your creativity even further and imagine you are floating into this other person's body, seeing the world through his or her eyes and feeling through his or her senses.

How do they stand? What are their typical facial expressions? How do they move? How do they speak? What clothes do they wear?

This exercise will help you to gain an understanding of the skills you need and the confidence to use them. We greatly underestimate our own abilities, and often all that is necessary to release them is a change in our perspective. If you are feeling brave, and I hope you are, why not take this exercise to the next level?

As you lie in bed, and just before you fall asleep, instruct your unconscious mind to meet this role model as you sleep and dream.

Many people throughout history have used this technique and attest to its benefits. So see what happens—you have nothing to lose.

Now you are ready to develop even more of your own visualizations, in different areas of your life, and join the lucky people. This is sufficient for now and is a natural point to end this chapter.

Now, review your notes and thoughts on this chapter. Ask yourself this question: "What three things can I do now that can help me immediately, or at least in the very near future, to make more luck playing poker?" Write your three points below.

In the next chapter, we will continue our journey and examine the critical importance of developing mindfulness when playing poker and how it can help us to get lucky.

In a Nutshell—Three Nuggets

1.

2.

3.

4

Mindfulness

As I start to write each chapter in this book, I think to myself, "This is the most important secret." The truth is that there are only seven secrets in my system, and so all of them are absolutely critical. Adopt any one, and you will probably attract more luck into your life and become a better poker player for it. However, adopt all seven secrets, and the effect will be magnified exponentially.

There is a huge reward waiting for those few who make the effort to learn the techniques of mindfulness. This reward manifests because developing mindfulness puts you in harmony with your unconscious mind; it allows you to flow, know yourself, let go, see the signs, and release more mind power than you ever believed possible.

Mindfulness works because it helps to create a calm mind. A calm mind gives room to the unconscious mind so that it can thrive, and it produces flow.

Mindfulness is the foundation for building what you want for your life, not what others think you deserve.

It should come as no surprise that mindfulness is gaining increasing popularity as a mind-tuning technique. I use it, one way or another, with every single client. Patients in hospitals and children in schools are learning it, and the technique is part of management development curricula for business executives. All poker players should learn it too.

Thinking too much should carry a health warning. My client, Rory Brown, no doubt agrees:

> In poker, though, there is no physical element. There is time to think. Endless time to second- guess and let fear of failure cloud judgment. Poker is about a series of decisions. Though luck plays an obvious part, players will win over the long term if they make the correct decisions.
>
> It is when the pressure is on—be it playing at a final table at your monthly game or at a major final table with millions of dollars at stake—that it can be extremely difficult to get a hold of one's own mind and make the correct decisions.[3]

Indeed, it can.

Mindfulness has helped so many people get lucky that it is deservedly secret number four. It is relatively easy to define, but it is far more difficult to explain why mindfulness can be of so much benefit and how it should be used.

Few would argue with this *Oxford Dictionaries* online definition for *mindfulness*: "A mental state achieved by focusing one's awareness on the present moment, while calmly acknowledging and accepting one's feelings, thoughts, and bodily sensations, used as a therapeutic technique." The last few words—"used as a therapeutic technique"—pose a number of important questions, particularly, "How can I use this technique to improve both the quality and consistency of my decisions when playing poker?"

Emotions Are Good but Not When Playing Poker

Before I attempt to answer this question, it will be helpful to discover just a little more about how our brains work, especially with regard to our emotions. Emotions can be helpful or unhelpful. When you play poker, it is great to feel confident and relaxed; it is not helpful to have doubts, fears, or envy, because they will destroy mindfulness. Look around any poker table and you will probably find all of these emotions on display.

As self-development writer and lecturer Dale Carnegie reasoned, it is important to recognize that "when dealing with people, you are not dealing with creatures of logic, but creatures of emotion."[11] So whether we like it or not, our emotions are here for good.

The challenge for us is how to have more helpful emotions and fewer unhelpful ones.

Before I even attempt to provide a solution for your consideration, I will add more detail to this challenge.

House of Cards

Our minds are almost constantly in states of utter chaos, so it's no wonder the quality of our decisions is often a lot less than we wish. Our thoughts are riddled with doubt, guilt, and uncertainty. We commonly hear ourselves and others complain that we are of two minds about the right thing to do. If only! Normally, many more options than that are competing for our attention. I am sure this is very familiar to you from your experiences as a poker player.

Ignorance is not a lack of ability to see the world as it is but a disregard of what our senses and thoughts are telling us. The reality is that we have millions of different thoughts competing for our attention at any one time—as if a council is in session inside our heads.

Its members represent every possible shade of political opinion, and we usually hear the member who shouts the loudest.

This helps to explain why we can reach two or more completely different decisions on the same subject within hours or even seconds of one another.

The ultimate goal of developing mindfulness is a quiet mind. Inside this tranquil head, the council converses softly, the members examine and debate an issue from every angle and take turns to speak, the others listen intently, consensus builds slowly, and the wisest member speaks last. When your mind becomes like this, you will start to play great poker.

You cannot control the cards, but you can control how to use them.

Our Brain—the Tip of the Iceberg

Also keep in mind that the brain remains one of the last barriers to scientists. Neurophysiologists have barely begun to unravel its secrets. What we do know is that we use but a fraction of the brain's potential. Some parts of our brains are rusty; others we have forgotten how to use. As with any part of the body or mind, we must use it or lose it. This includes the control of our emotions.

So what are emotions, and why do we have them?

Emotions and gut feelings are shortcuts that the brain uses to process huge amounts of information and chunk them down to a more manageable size.

This is hugely important. The most common shortcuts our brains use to condense information are generalization, deletion, and distortion. The advantage in using these shortcuts is that they will speed up your thoughts and decisions. You will know how important this is as a poker player. The disadvantage in using them is that very often you will not understand why you acted in a certain way. The unhelpful, adrenaline-fueled emotions, such as fear and even excitement, will magnify the effects of generalizing, deleting, and distorting our thoughts. This is why you might have experienced the same situation another day and acted in a completely different way.

Think back to some of your recent poker sessions. Does this sound familiar? The good news is that mindfulness increases our awareness of our emotions, and this recognition allows us to exert a degree of control over not only our neurotransmitters but also our responses to them.

If I thought it was easy to develop mindfulness, then I would say so. It is not, but a little more of it can go a very long way indeed.

Remember that most players you go up against will have much less mindfulness than you.

Their chips are yours; it is only a matter of time and having just a little more luck. Over the long term, mindful people are more likely to attract luck than those who are not.

Your Onboard Computer Has Limits

Our brains are like computers. We can handle only so much information at any one time. When our brains are overloaded, they slow down or even freeze—much like the Windows Blue Screen of Death.

Computers work fastest and are most reliable when only one program is running because then there is less chance of software incompatibility. Of course, our brains are vastly more powerful than computers and will continue to be so for the foreseeable future, but they still have their limits. They too work best when only a few programs are open.

A conscientious computer owner runs only the programs that are in use at any given time and defragments the hard disk regularly to free up space and increase processing power. Few people take the same care with their brain, which is why they lose themselves in the background noise. Overloading your brain puts you at risk of not being able to find some of your most precious gifts—it leads to too much noise and not enough signal.

The German-born painter Hans Hofmann was one of those rare individuals who could combine the rigorous disciplines of science and mathematics with abstract expressionist art and still find time to think. Perhaps his secret to success was an exceptionally ordered mind. His approach was one of ruthless simplification: "The ability to simplify means to eliminate the unnecessary so that the necessary may speak."[12] In other words, allow room for the unconscious mind to speak.

While it might appear that our brains are unlimited in their power, they do have limits; while it is true they possess enormous memory and can handle huge amounts of data, they nevertheless have some boundaries. Scientists have established that our brains can process only seven items of information at any one time. Once this limit is exceeded, the pure information is corrupted. While the content remains identical at a deep level, the overlying abbreviated information could become quite different.

This is not what we need when playing poker.

Back to the Swamp

Another problem we face is that our emotions are rooted in the murky depths of our reptilian brains, where our most primitive reflexes are hard-wired. These reflexes are information shortcuts and have evolutionary importance inasmuch as they can be directly linked to our survival, which is why we still have them.

When Mr. Caveman is confronted by a saber-toothed tiger, he does not have time to consider all the details of his situation. Fight or flight—that is the only decision he has time to make, and he needs to make it right away. If he were to think of too many options at the same time, then he would freeze, paralyzed by fear—the worst possible outcome. We have all frozen at some time, and it is not a pleasant feeling. It is not as bad as being eaten by a tiger, though.

Fighting, fleeing, and freezing are primitive reflexes that can destroy your playing performance. They have no place in your game plan, and a far better objective is to remain as emotionally neutral as possible. I know this is easier said than done, which is why developing a state of mindfulness will be so valuable.

Mindfulness = concentration = good decisions = more chips.

Distractions and Attention Leaks

Genius poker is played with a calm mind, but unfortunately, our normal state of mind is chaotic. This chaos should not come as a surprise, considering that we are now surrounded by so much up-to-the-second information, which bombards us from the TV, radio, and newspapers; social media contacts; breaking news on our smartphones; text messages; telephones; diary reminders; and e-mails 24/7.

Unless we can reduce these attention leaks, the quality of our poker will take a huge change for the worse.

When we receive information, the processing choices open to our brain are simple, as there are only three: We can act on information, file it away, or delete it. This requires concentration, and we require it when it is necessary to make important decisions on the basis of complex information.

As a matter of fact, concentration involves the effective mobilization of an exquisite balance of both conscious and unconscious thought. Contrary to what we might say to others, we do not lose our concentration. At any one time, there are simply too many places for it to go. It is not lost; it has just gone somewhere else.

There is a lot to think about when playing poker, and not much time. So any distraction will have exceeded your capacity to process seven packets of information at any one time. The result is likely to be a lack of concentration, leading to poor decision-making, a sense of energy draining away, and the pleasure of the moment being lost forever. The problem is that many players believe they can multitask effectively and become rather vociferous when challenged on this subject.

So what are the distractions most likely to destroy mindfulness when you are playing poker? Whether you play poker online, in a casino, or at an event, there are many distractions and attention leaks.

Jot them down; you will be surprised by how many you can think of.

At an event, spend some time walking around the tables and note the distracted players. I do, and I am amazed by the number of players denying themselves the possibility of playing anywhere near their best. It is the equivalent of playing with a stacked deck. Do not be one of these players—just take their chips.

Now, it is time to explain exactly how to do this. The following tips are pretty simple, but I know they can also be quite a challenge for most of us.

Quick Tips to Be More Mindful Now

In a nutshell, if you want to be more mindful, then it is critical that you process only the minimum amount of information required to make a decision. So how can you limit the information you allow in? Just stop doing all the things you note other players doing when you walk around the tables.

I suggested you list some of these behaviors. Did they include engaging with other players any more than necessary, checking the other players' chip counts, texting, ordering food, and sending social media updates? Avoid these distractions, and turn your electronic gadgets off (other than for listening to music, as this can be very beneficial).

Performers know that nothing breaks a flowing presentation, the creation of a beautiful work of art, or the straight flight of an arrow more certainly than a single thought.

Quite simply, multitasking does not work. You will almost certainly be painfully surprised by how difficult it is to turn off all your information-gathering gadgets. When was the last time you turned them off for more than twelve hours? Many people struggle with turning them off for twelve minutes.

Adopting these tips will not result in any permanent positive changes overnight. A month seems to be about the minimum time required to cement a change in behavior, which means that one month is the minimum time you will need to commit. By then, any benefits should be clear, and you will not want to go back to your previous situation. The German philosopher Hans Margolius doubtless agreed with this assessment when he wrote, "Only in quiet waters do things mirror themselves undistorted. Only in a quiet mind is adequate perception of the world."[13]

So increased perception when playing poker is almost within our grasp. I call this intuition, and it is priceless; surely it must be worth the effort.

Keep It Simple

If you have any doubts about your ability or resolve to take action and banish multitasking from your life, then the following example should provide some comfort.

Mindfulness is your natural state and has existed from the time of your birth, if not before.

The problem is that, over the years, your natural state has developed into an emotional state. For the best possible reasons, you have allowed your conscious mind far too much control, and now you are thinking of too many unnecessary and unimportant things. If you want great examples of mindfulness, then study your pets. Your dogs, cats, horses, parakeets, and even goldfish are probably more mindful than you because they live in the now.

So developing mindfulness is a conundrum. You do not require any new tools because you already have them; instead, your challenge is in returning to the human being you used to be before other people or your experiences complicated your life.

Give Your Brain a Holiday

The best way to find out just how much these distractive barriers apply to you and prevent you from developing mindfulness is to put them to the test. Indeed, it is the only way. If you have the time and money, then go away for six months. Find some place without Internet, TV, radio, or newspapers—not an easy mission in today's world!

Few except for the truly fortunate can afford a six-month sabbatical. Many more, however, can manage two weeks, a week, a long weekend, or even just two days. So go ahead and try it. I did, and I found the experience a lot more disturbing than I thought it would be. See for yourself.

When sensory input is reduced and much of what remains is directly in tune with our life goals, the energy will surely flow.

Who can guess what other magical things might happen to you? What difference would this make to your poker playing? To your life?

Throughout this chapter, we have explored the chaotic mess that we call our brain. If it were a trash can, then we would have no way to close the lid on it because of its overflowing contents. Much of this garbage is worthless even though we may not know it. Unfortunately, the precious gold nuggets that often hide within this waste may be lost from sight forever. What better time than now for a thorough spring-cleaning?

You could do worse than follow K. T. Jong's advice to turn down the volume. Less noise equates to more signal: "It is only when we silent the blaring sounds of our daily existence that we can finally hear the whispers of truth that life reveals to us, as it stands knocking on the doorsteps of our hearts."[14] The more information you move from the conscious to the unconscious areas of your brain, the higher your performance level will be. This is true for any area of your life, whether at home, in sports, or at work.

Now, review your notes and thoughts on this chapter. Ask yourself this question: "What three things can I do now that can help me immediately, or at least in the very near future, to make more luck playing poker?" Write your three points below.

Give yourself sufficient time to digest these thoughts. Some of them might be uncomfortable because much of this chapter was about what *not* to do to become mindful. The next chapter will focus on several far more positive strategies that will be fun and definitely produce incredible results in certain lucky people.

In a Nutshell—Three Nuggets

1.

2.

3.

5

The Three *H*s of Havening, Heartmath, and Hypnosis

How to Find the Zone Faster and Stay There Longer

The three Hs of Havening, HeartMath, and hypnosis are the most powerful weapons in my armory, and they comprise the fifth secret to getting lucky. Used together, they have helped to produce some incredible results in my clients. You owe it to yourself to learn at least a little more about each of them; any one could transform the way you think about poker and raise your game at least one level.

All three of these techniques have their supporters and skeptics. The science that supports them is incomplete and sometimes controversial. However, I do not recommend any product or technique unless I have used it myself and enjoyed its benefits.

I practice each of these techniques daily and believe that more information is well worth your consideration.

When used as mind-expanding tools, Havening, HeartMath, and hypnosis have much in common with one another and are closely related to meditation. Where they differ is that meditation is a universal technique that provides an overall calm and focused mind, whereas Havening, HeartMath, and hypnosis can be used for specific problems when facilitated by a trained therapist. In other words, meditation hits the target, but the three *H*s fly straight for the bull's-eye.

Finding a Safe Place

Dr. Ron Ruden founded the Havening Technique. I met him when self-development guru Paul McKenna introduced us and have since had the privilege to work with him on many occasions.

A relatively new technique, Havening is described as a psychosensory therapy involving touch that uses sensory input to change the neurochemical wiring in a deep part of the reptilian brain. Mothers are often perfect examples of this as they unconsciously use the Havening touch with their children. As a matter of fact, it is a natural reflex to comfort another person. Havening is particularly effective in treating post-traumatic stress disorders, but it is also effective in treating a wide range of neurological disorders, including phobias, panic attacks, addictions, and chronic pain.

This is how it works: Threats perceived through our five senses enter a deep part of the brain called the thalamus, where they are processed. If perceived as imminently dangerous, they are then encoded in the amygdala. Threats received through the sense of smell, however, go straight to the amygdala for encoding. This exception is, presumably, an evolutionary shortcut adaptation, as fire may have been the most common direct threat to life in the early ages. The amygdala, which can be described as a mongoose on sentry duty, never sleeps and is always alert for potential danger.

The problem is that sometimes an event can be perceived as dangerous when, in reality, it is quite trivial.

Trivial events that were miscoded in childhood can exert strong negative influences throughout one's adult life—and miscoding is far more common than one would expect. It is something I always check for, as treatment can have profound beneficial effects.

Children often feel vulnerable, and these memories may linger into adulthood. The adult knows these feelings are no longer appropriate, but the reptilian brain is not logical, so these memories continue to generate inappropriate and dangerous effects.

I use Havening with almost every client because, in the majority of cases, they all have at least one traumatic event that was once encoded.

Releasing the fear and other emotions from this event is always the first step. When the client describes the euphoric feeling of letting go, I can then move forward to explore future goals and identify the resources the client will require to reach them. There really is no limit to the creativity with which Havening can be used, and I use it in a wide variety of different circumstances. In summary, Havening is a way to move forward from the past and paint such a vivid picture of the future that the client begins to lead a life of self-fulfilling prophecies. By its action deep within the brain negative emotions are detached from the memories of past traumatic events. These memories are not forgotten. They are put into context as past events that carry no threat in the present time.

There are numerous instructional videos on YouTube that demonstrate the Havening Technique; however, as you would expect, there is no substitute for working with an appropriately qualified therapist. Indeed, it can be dangerous not to do so.

Finding a Coherent Place

HeartMath is also a relatively new technique and a form of meditation. The benefits of regular meditation are well established in science, and in my opinion, every poker player should use some form of meditation during play, especially during the player's most important hands. The benefits include reducing anxiety, lowering high blood pressure, and even lessening the risk of cancer. For these reasons and others, HeartMath is increasingly being used in professional sports, businesses, and schools to enhance performance and help to create the ideal mental state.

Poker presents many challenges to creating the ideal mental state, including too much time to think and periods of high emotional pressure. This is why HeartMath is such a valuable technique for poker players to learn.

The heart contains large amounts of nerves. Scientists previously thought these nerves responded to stimulation from the brain but now know the reverse is often true—that is, the impulses from the heart control the brain. This might explain why people use the expression "I knew in my head that this was the right decision, but in my heart, I knew it was wrong." I am sure your poker career is full of these or similar experiences that demonstrate the importance of intuition.

People perform best at work, school, sports, or any creative activity when they reach a balance between the challenge of the task and their mental state. If the challenge is low, then their mental state is likely to be one of boredom, and their performance will be poor. If the challenge is balanced in conjunction with a calm mind, then the individual will move into that magical state known as the zone—the home of peak performance. However, if the challenge is too high, then this causes stress and an associated loss of confidence.

Players make poor decisions when playing because they have too many thoughts at one time.

Any tool that can help a player to find the zone more easily and stay in it longer is of immense value. And this is exactly what HeartMath delivers when used correctly. It is noteworthy that Chris Moorman scored strongly when he mastered this technique shortly before his first live-event victory.

The ideal mental state depends on the ability of the individual to strengthen positive emotions and minimize negative ones. It is an incredibly complex balance, with over fourteen hundred known biochemical changes affecting it.

The core of HeartMath is finding the perfectly balanced relationship between the heart and the brain. The brain is packed with nerve cells, which is why it controls the rest of the body with perfect precision. Less known is that there are also numerous nerve cells in and around the heart; even lesser known is the stunning fact that these nerve cells send more information to the brain than the other way around.

Therefore, the brain is not controlling the heart, but the heart is controlling the brain.

Using this knowledge, you can apply the HeartMath technique in your life and in poker to enhance your mental state and hence promote your peak performance.

The HeartMath technique is based upon the concept of heart rate variability. For example, if your heart rate is sixty, then your heart beats once every second. However, it is not quite as simple as that because during any five-second period, the heart may beat five times. But it is also quite likely that the heart may beat only four times or as many as six. So heart rate is only the average number of beats in a sixty-second period. This variation between individual heartbeats is called the heart rate variability.

Heart rate variability is dependent upon our age; general state of health; and most importantly, our mental state. High heart rate variability produces positive emotions while the opposite is true of low heart rate variability. So how can we increase our heart rate variability and find the ideal mental state, known as coherence? The answer is to practice specific breathing techniques. These techniques, which lead to a higher level of coherence, are very simple, and yet they still produce great results.

There are also more complex HeartMath techniques, some of which are computerized. They are particularly helpful because they provide a second-by-second recording of your mental state. Even though I have practiced them every day for many years, I am still learning how to achieve better coherence scores.

The following breathing technique is a great way to start understanding how to use HeartMath. We have already stressed the importance of the heart; to start this exercise, bring your attention to the area around your heart. Breathe rhythmically, and at the same time, imagine that your breath is going into and then leaving your heart. Breathe in for five seconds and breathe out for five seconds. Perform this exercise for five minutes or even less, and you will feel much calmer. The truth is that it is very difficult to be calm when you are breathing quickly, and it is even more difficult to be anxious when you are breathing slowly.

I have mentioned the importance of emotions to our state of mind many times. So your next challenge is to use the simple technique described above again, but this time add a magical ingredient to the mix—a positive emotion. Think of a person you love who loves you. Think of a time when your life was easy and you were in the zone, performing at a much higher level than normal. Think of how you would like to feel in the future and about the goals you would like to achieve in your life.

Finally, think of how good this achievement will make you feel. While you are generating these positive emotions and chemicals, focus your mind at the same time on the feeling of breathing through your heart. Just as before, breathe in for five seconds and breathe out for five seconds.

The HeartMath Institute has an extremely informative website (https://www.heartmath.org), and much of its content is freely available. It is well worth a visit. In addition, more compelling HeartMath research findings, especially those published in the booklet *Science of the Heart*, provide much food for thought. In any case, the message is clear: HeartMath is a form of meditation that anyone can practice. As the benefits are now beyond dispute, any form of meditation is well worth your consideration.

Finding a Deep Place

Hypnosis is often referred to as the "*H* word" because it has such negative connotations among certain people. I do not fully understand why this is so, but perhaps there needs to be a clearer distinction between stage hypnosis and the therapeutic hypnosis that I practice. In a nutshell, hypnosis is the fastest, most effective technique that I know to connect to the unconscious mind.

We are surrounded by examples of hypnosis—and everybody can be a hypnotist, although some will be better than others. One of the best examples is the natural way with which a mother soothes her troubled child. Many commercials we see on TV are also hypnotic, whether their creators know it or not. Politicians are experts, and many do know it.

I can guarantee one thing: You will be confused by hypnosis. If you are a hypnotist, if you are hypnotized, or if you are a student of hypnosis, then you know the more you study hypnosis, the more confused you will become. I can only hope that it is confusion at a deeper level of understanding.

Hypnosis forms the foundation of my work with my clients. I learned much from legendary self-help gurus Paul McKenna and Richard Bandler, but I have probably been a hypnotist all my life. I experimented on my mother when I was a teenager, and she had such a strong reaction that

I was too terrified to hypnotize another person for many years. I now know that this reaction is called an "abreaction" and is a relatively common occurrence. Webster's definition of abreaction is "the expression and emotional discharge of unconscious material". With the wisdom of twenty-twenty retrospective hindsight, I can categorically state that no one should hypnotize another person unless he or she is confident and competent in his or her ability to handle an abreaction.

In 2007, my career was at a crossroads due to increasing pain and disability from an earlier neck injury. I clearly could not continue the grueling travel schedule and emergency response that was an essential part of my job, so what were my options? Fortunately, I was young enough to start a new career in the subject that had always fascinated me—psychology. I was, however, not young enough to return to a university and earn another master's degree, let alone have enough time to build a client base and grow my experience.

I needed accelerated learning, and the best way to learn fast was to study with the best.

You cannot do much better than to train with Richard Bandler and Paul McKenna, as both are regarded as world experts in self-development and hypnosis.

According to the literature, hypnosis is induced by a series of preliminary instructions and suggestions. These can be lengthy and complicated, and I have even seen some hypnotists reading their induction script from a detailed checklist. I can only give my opinion, and I apologize if it contradicts other views that may be equally valid or even more so, but I do not use formal hypnotic inductions. The nearest I come to a formal induction is to sit quietly in meditation, without speaking, for a few minutes before I start talking to my client.

Light hypnosis can be achieved within seconds and deep hypnosis within another minute or two. It is not necessary to reach a state of deep hypnosis to perform deep hypnotherapy. Sometimes even a light trance produces more spectacular results. That said, hypnosis should be seen as an art and used sparingly.

I do not know how hypnosis works its magic. But I do know it is a deeply relaxing or meditative state of mind whereby the busy conscious mind is quieted so that the deeper thoughts from the unconscious mind can surface. I do not know in what area of the brain hypnosis produces its effects either. Increasing evidence suggests that the nerve cells of the brain are "plastic." In other words, these cells are malleable: cells normally devoted to vision, for instance, can change their function. In a blind person, these cells may become sound receptor cells so that they can provide a different sensory input to aid that person.

New and complex neural pathways are created and destroyed all the time. Sooner or later, the network reaches its optimum route, and a process called myelination kicks in. Myelin is the protective sheath that surrounds and nourishes the neuron. The more this neuron is used the more myelin sheathes it, and the faster the nerve can conduct an impulse. An example would be when a child learns to ride a bike; most of the early neural pathways result in the child falling off the bike until something magical connects. After this, the child will remember how to ride a bike for the rest of his or her life and do so without even consciously thinking about it.

It is likely that hypnosis works its magic by establishing communication with the deeper layers of the brain, which makes it possible to learn skills much faster than when using willpower and traditional methods of coaching. So for the foreseeable future, hypnosis will raise more questions than answers; however, its effects can certainly be very powerful and incredibly beneficial. One thing I know for sure: hypnosis can definitely attract more luck into your life, as many of my clients have discovered.

It's much easier to see Havening, HeartMath, and hypnosis in action or even talk about them than to read about them. You'll see further information on how to get started on this in the conclusion.

Now, review your notes and thoughts on this chapter. Ask yourself this question: "What three things can I do now that can help me immediately, or at least in the very near future, to make more luck playing poker?" Write your three points below.

If this chapter was not confusing enough, the next chapter will examine luck from several other different angles. Some of these will be eminently sensible while others will border on the absurd. One thing is certain: its conclusions will raise at least a few more niggling questions in your mind about whether we truly live in a totally random universe, how you might be able to use this information, and what effect it could have on your results.

In a Nutshell—Three Nuggets

1.

2.

3.

6

The Benefits of Logic

THE SIXTH SECRET to getting lucky when playing poker is to use logic and make it your friend. Or more precisely, it is how you can attract more luck into your poker playing by being a luck magnet. Is this possible? It should be. And in theory, this secret should be the easiest for you to master because there are a number of logical reasons for it. We will cover some of these reasons in this chapter. Supporters of this secret claim there are also some extremely illogical reasons for attracting luck. These are more difficult to explain, however, and will be covered in the next chapter.

I spoke to many people about luck while researching this book. An expression I heard often was, "The harder I work, the luckier I get." This is true because we have to work at everything in life. Still, very few people achieve great success without considerable effort, yet many spend their whole lives working very hard with little luck and success to show for it, particularly compared with those who work a lot less and are a lot luckier.

You Do Not Need to Spend Ten Years in Jail, Though It Helps

In conversation and in print, I have often come across the "theory of ten thousand hours." Apparently, it takes at least ten thousand hours of deep practice to become an expert at anything. That is a lot of poker hands that you are going to have to grind through!

Without a doubt, there is a lot of truth in this statement. But it is quoted as if it is the whole truth when nothing could be further from it. The reason this statement worries me is that it can be a powerful, negative, self-fulfilling prophecy. It also does not give enough credit to innate talent or the power of accelerated learning delivered by skillful coaching.

How many people will be discouraged from learning a new skill when they figure that ten thousand hours of deep practice will take them at least ten years to clock?

The ten-thousand-hours story first surfaced in a paper published by K. Anders Ericsson and his colleagues in 1993. It is a brilliant paper—forty-four pages long, extremely technical, and definitely not an easy read, which might be why its conclusions are not as clear as some might believe. When writing a scientific paper, the biggest challenge for the author is to eliminate what statisticians call confounding factors. These can skew the results and lead to faulty conclusions.

Let me explain: Do you think that a kid who clocks ten thousand hours of deep violin practice is going to be the average kid who lives next door and has average parents with an average income and an average interest in music? I don't think so. And to be fair, neither did Ericsson and his colleagues. They were the first to accept that their elegant paper raised a lot more questions than answers. Of course, this talented and conscientious kid wholly deserves our respect. But I'm more interested in the kid from the inner city who does not have the same advantages but improvises and finds other ways that allow his or her talent to surface—the kid who has fun and experiments but does not take ten thousand hours to become an expert.

Having said all that, all the players I work with have put in their ten thousand hours. They are mainly in their midtwenties and early thirties. My prediction is that they will continue to improve as long as they keep themselves physically and mentally fit. The other consideration is that, as they are all intelligent and highly motivated people, they may find other opportunities to exercise their skills. Not that there is any sign of this at the moment—they all love poker and their lifestyles and have no plans to do anything different anytime soon.

Do As They Do

More good news in our search for luck reveals that researchers have identified a consistent pattern among people who lead lucky lives. These people are often extroverted and hence attract many friends. They have large social networks and are, therefore, often the first to hear of new opportunities. They are social magnets, and they are luck magnets too. This is all unlikely to be coincidence.

Another characteristic of lucky people is their relaxed attitude toward life; they are more likely to see all of the options available to them in any situation. This is in stark contrast to anxious people, who focus on internal rather than external issues and so never recognize these opportunities. Lucky people also have more open minds, and this seems to be particularly important. Often they share an unconventional outlook on life as well. This is probably not too surprising, and this opinion certainly applies to some of the people I know.

Success and luck are inextricably linked, and successful people often identify their ability to see unusual opportunities that others do not as a strength. Others miss these opportunities because they do not fit the pattern they expect to see. This is the same reason why most people struggle to spot a hologram on first occasion. After initial processing, the visual cortex rejects the hologram because it is so different from a normal image; this rejection occurs because the image does not fit the expected and well-developed innate pattern-recognition criteria we all possess.

Do As They Do Not

We can always learn something from other people. In the previous section, we examined the people who have most of the critical success factors. What about those who do not have these factors? For example, cynical people are usually not lucky people.

Luckily for me, the majority of my clients are not cynical. This is prob-ably because they are a self-selected group; most people do not take the time and trouble to find a mind coach, so my clients are not a represen-tative cross-sectional sample. This is another example of a confounding factor, just like the musicians Ericsson studied.

While these clients are not cynical, some do have doubts when we start to work together.

They might have doubts about whether they are they good enough to succeed. They might have doubts about me, and whether my techniques good enough.

I fully understand these doubts and am aware that they have surfaced for some underlying reason. So I explore the clients' past experiences and usually identify a small number of incidents that have disproportion-ately colored their outlooks on life. Then I can focus on techniques that remind my clients of all the great things they have achieved and wonder-ful people they have met. This allows them to put into perspective their previous bad experiences and the people who let them down. I then move on, and these clients do at least as well as the others.

In a previous chapter, we talked about visualization, and now we defi-nitely know that lucky people have big dreams. Some of these dreams will never be realized, and the cynics will enjoy pointing this out; other dreams, however, will come true, because the more often you position yourself for success, the more likely it is that you will succeed at some point.

Another pitfall to avoid is becoming too content after a lucky experi-ence. Good luck materializing out of the blue can be frightening to some people. On occasion, it has even been frightening for me too, so I can understand why some players would feel this way. A common expression such people use is this: "I'm going to take it easy now because I don't want to push my luck too far." However, when lucky people are on a roll, they don't stop riding the wave; they keep dreaming big and fully expect their good luck to continue in the future. Even in adverse situations, they truly believe it is only a matter of time before the tide will turn and their luck will change.

When the Going Gets Tough, the Tough Get Going

And so, even lucky people face adversity at some point in their lives. But once again, their attitude toward it is very different from that of unlucky people. Poker players know this better than most: The odds are often stacked against Lady Luck, and the dreaded tilt is never too far away. Still, lucky people are convinced that, however bad things may be now, all will work out for the best sooner or later. They truly feel the experience will make them stronger; moreover, they do not blame themselves or others for their misfortune and move on to the future far more rapidly than most people.

The unlucky people, however, give up in the face of adversity—sometimes when they are a lot closer to their goal than they realize.

Adversity is a serious subject and extremely important in determining whether you will be a luck magnet. It is not a topic we like to think about too much, but it is how we deal with adversity that determines our level of happiness (or lack thereof) and whether or not we will attract luck. Like it or not, we will all face adversity at some point in our lives—sudden sickness, loss of employment, poor housing conditions, limited income, work stress, and much more. But whatever the situation, we can call upon certain role-model behaviors as needed.

One of the irritating clichés people use is this: "Don't worry. Good will come from adversity." These people mean well, but their comments do not seem helpful at the time. However, when we look back, they are often right. Very few great successes in life happen easily; in fact, they are mostly preceded by months or years of increasing frustration. Another often-heard cliché is, "It was hard to believe at the time, but it was probably the best thing that ever happened to me!"

Poker and poetry form an unusual combination, but I wonder if Quintus Horatius Flaccus—one of the leading Roman poets at the time of Augustus—was a card player, because he was thinking along lines that could be useful for a player when he said, "Adversity has the effect of eliciting talents that, in prosperous circumstances, would have lain dormant."[15]

Good Luck or Bad Luck?

You may have heard of bad-luck–good-luck stories. I suggest you make a note about your most significant cases of bad luck. It will almost certainly be very illuminating. In retrospect, did these events result in positive outcomes?

I have been lucky throughout my life and can remember only three occasions when luck seriously deserted me. In comparison to many people's experiences, these misfortunes are somewhat trivial—but at the time, they were extremely stressful. My first bad experience was in 1990, my second in 1999, and the most recent in 2007. They are all examples of bad-luck–good-luck stories. I will not bore you with the details, but these episodes were pivotal; they all changed my life immeasurably for the better, although it did not feel so at the time. I would not turn the clock back, even if I could.

This is a good time for you to contemplate your bad-luck–good-luck stories. The time you spend now may be richly rewarded later.

Now, review your notes and thoughts on this chapter. Ask yourself this question: "What three things can I do now that can help me immediately, or at least in the very near future, to make more luck playing poker?" Write your three points below.

This chapter explored the reasons why some people are luckier than others and tried to unravel the thread of logic that connects these thin strands of evidence. We will test these same strands to their limits in the next chapter as we explore the world of the unknown unknowns. Prepare yourself for a bumpy ride.

In a Nutshell—Three Nuggets

1.

2.

3.

7

Mind Magic

GIVE YOU FAIR warning: This chapter will make your brain hurt. It will be worth the pain, though, because the incredible successes my clients and I have enjoyed just might be explained by magic. Successes like that of the golfer scoring not just one, but an incredible six holes in one.

However, this is a book about poker, and while we have enjoyed its many twists and turns, we are almost home free. The journey ends where it started, with Chris Moorman staring at defeat and appealing to the poker gods for an ace on the "river", the final community card in Texas Hold'em. He was poised to win his first major live event if he could get lucky—very lucky indeed. It was down to the final three players, but Chris would be out soon unless his luck changed. A pair of 10s helped, but he needed something more.

Just in case brick is a new word to you, it refers to a card that is not likely to be helpful. Chris tells this story better than I can:

> We had to wait, for what felt like an eternity, for the flop to be dealt. Finally, it came down K-Q-J, which kept everyone in the hunt. Glenn Lafaye would win the tournament if the turn and river bricked out; Michael needed a 10 and a brick to cripple me and all but make it to heads up play between just the two of us, and I needed an ace, a 9, and a brick, or a 10 and a board pair that

wasn't a queen or jack to make it to heads up play, even stacked with Glenn.

The turn also took an age to deal, and all I can remember was a huge brick.

> *About five seconds before the dealer dealt the river, I felt this strong wave of positivity inside me, and I uttered the words "Barry Greenstein" to myself repeatedly. And then, to my astonishment, it came: ace on the river! "Get in!"*

For your information Barry Greenstein wrote the illuminating book *Ace on the River*. So Chris had his A-K-Q-J-10. He was not likely to make any more mistakes, and sure enough, the title was soon his. So what possible explanation could there be for this good fortune other than random variance?

The previous chapter focused on the direct-line-of-sight logic that explains why some people have more luck than others. All we have to do is do what they do, and then we will attract more luck too. But if you agree with my mantra that the enemy of the best is the good, then you will also agree that we want more than just a little more good luck—we want mountains of it. In this chapter, we will look at the far more esoteric origins of luck. Whether we will be able to use them is less certain but definitely possible. For want of a better word, I call this subject magic.

According to *Oxford Dictionaries*, one definition of magic is "the power of apparently influencing events by using mysterious or supernatural forces."[16] My definition of magic is more abstract: To me, it is a perfect cocktail of luck and intuition. I do not believe luck is random, but I do believe magic has a scientific basis. One day, we will discover its origin. However, we do not have to wait for an explanation; fortunately, we can use magic without understanding its source.

Chris called upon luck for his final card, known as the river card, just as previous generations have done because they, too, want to believe in luck. It is not clear why so many of us want to believe in luck, but one plausible explanation is that this desire just might arise from a deep fear of living in an environment where the individual has little control over external events. Is this fear of the future programmed into our genes? Or is it a behavior we learned from others and our own experiences?

The answer is probably a combination of all of it. A certain amount of foresight and planning for the future would give humans an edge over other species in terms of survival. We are warm-blooded and do not possess hide or hair protection to the degree other creatures do, so we need to prepare for the cold months to survive.

At a conscious level, we identify what we want to control in our lives. If we cannot or do not wish to exert this control ourselves, then we find others to do so by proxy. At an unconscious level, it is far simpler: we just do it.

A run of winning results brings with it a euphoric emotional high that can be addictive. Enjoying the sense of mastery over external events is heady stuff, and it is not only poker players who have fallen prey to its beguiling nature.

Poker is certainly a game of skill based on statistics, analysis of hand histories, and human factors, many of which I have already described in this book. However, luck enters the equation too, for sure. And experienced players carefully manage their bankrolls to smooth its variances. Over the long term, luck regresses to the mean, and the wide swings in both directions balance one another out. That said, your bankroll needs to be sufficient to cope with prolonged losing rounds because you should definitely expect them.

Trust the Universe to Deliver

Universal laws have many supporters and provide another explanation. For instance, many people now talk about universal laws—especially the law of attraction—as the ultimate form of control. This law proposes that our conscious and unconscious thoughts can influence external events. The best-selling documentary *The Secret* (The Secret, http://www.thesecret.tv.)

describes the law of attraction in more detail. It was released in 2006 and became instantly popular.

Rightly or wrongly, the belief that "thoughts become things" resonated deeply with millions around the world. *The Secret* argued that all we have to do is "ask, believe, and receive" and then let the power of the universe take care of everything else. For some people, this is enough information, and they are probably already following this or a similar mantra. Others surely require more convincing. What explanation could they possibly get? If there is an answer, it is most likely hidden deep within the unconscious mind.

The law of attraction not only postulates that positive people attract other positive people, but it also says positive events attract further positive events. Indeed, the law goes even further to propose that positive thoughts can lead directly to positive events, even at considerable distances. If we can believe even a fraction of this statement, then the implications are immense. Many grounded and pragmatic people, who have never even heard of the law of attraction let alone put it into practice, believe that some strange force is out there working in their favor. The words they use include "luck," "coincidence," "synchronicity," "serendipity," "fate," and "karma." They often explain that a particular event was meant to be or that things just fell into place.

French surgeon Alexis Carrel won the Nobel Prize in Physiology or Medicine in 1912. To this day, transplant surgeons still use his techniques for rejoining blood vessels. Surgery is, by necessity, a practical specialty, but Carrel was a controversial freethinker too. He believed, for instance, that unseen forces can shape our destiny. He specifically mentioned intuition, a subject that has surfaced many times in this book already.

In the introduction, I wrote, "The overarching conclusion I reached writing this book was that luck is inextricably linked to intuition."

I wonder if that is what Carrel had in mind when he wrote, "Intuition comes very close to clairvoyance; it appears to be the extrasensory perception of reality."[17]

Show Me the Money

These ideas are not original. Napoleon Hill proposed similar theories in his book *Think and Grow Rich*, which was published in 1937 and remains a best seller, with over sixty million copies sold. At least it worked for Hill, as he became very rich. Many of his readers have been convinced it worked for them too.

Scientists now broadly accept the enormous influence and power of the unconscious mind, and yet their research has not begun to scratch the tip of this iceberg—indeed, not even the uppermost ice crystal. On the one hand, this is frustrating, but on the other hand, it means that your opinion is just about as valid as anybody else's. Perhaps the law of attraction is yet another example of the unseen power of the unconscious mind.

Eyes Wide Open

We already know we all miss a huge amount of vital information that is right in front of us—information that could change our lives. More accurately, we do not miss this information; we just fail to process it from our unconscious into our conscious minds. Or our processing is incomplete, which may lead to critical errors of interpretation.

A person's mind takes multiple huge shortcuts and largely "sees" what it expects to see on the basis of previous experiences. This is why it is so difficult to see a hologram for the first time, as I mentioned before. When we see, hear, or feel something so unusual that our conscious mind rejects it, the echo of this memory persists; it causes a feeling of uneasiness, similar to the irritation of an unfinished conversation, until it finds the right environment in which to surface—often, annoyingly, at four in the morning, when we are struggling to sleep.

As with any other skill, we can improve our intuition with practice. Poet and author Robert Graves knew its value: "Intuition is the supralogic that cuts out all the routine processes of thought and leaps straight from the problem to the answer."[18]

So how can you use all this contradictory and confusing information? Be prepared to experiment with different options. It is not likely that success will arise from repeating previously unsuccessful efforts. Indeed, Einstein has been attributed with defining insanity as doing the same thing repeatedly and expecting different results.

Trust your intuition and instincts, but always ask yourself, "What is the risk?" This is the safety net, because while instincts often turn out to be correct, we can spectacularly misplace them on occasion, with dire consequences.

Self-development guru Paul McKenna also believes we create our own luck and studies successful people to identify their secrets. He wrote, "Whether you choose to believe in the law of attraction or not, it's interesting to note that many highly successful people do."[19]

So these ideas absolutely merit further reflection, irrespective of their current lack of scientific basis. The law of attraction has provided lucky breaks for many of my clients and many of its other supporters too. It just might do the same for you.

There Is Nothing to Worry About

If you are not comfortable with universal laws, perhaps the world of science might have something more persuasive to explain how luck might not be random. You be the judge, so here goes.

According to quantum physics, all matter is made of almost completely nothing, and so are you. The majority of what appears to be a poker chip, an airplane, or even a person is really just empty space surrounding a small amount of matter.

Almost everything in the universe is nothing. If you could extract all the matter from our population, it would just about cover your thumbnail. Everything else is nothing—just empty space between the smallest subatomic particles. It is rather like staring up into the sky on a clear night, where the stars are the equivalent of our subatomic particles and the rest is empty space.

In one sense, however, this space is not empty; energy travels through it. This energy includes gravitational effects from stars. It also includes radio waves and radiation and all the other components of the electromagnetic spectrum. The only part of the spectrum you perceive is the tiny bit you can see, which is the visible light.

The two greatest breakthroughs in physics during the last century were the advances in the theories of relativity and quantum mechanics. Indeed, leading physicist Stephen Hawking wrote in *A Briefer History of Time*, "Today scientists describe the universe in terms of two basic partial theories—the general theory of relativity and quantum mechanics."[20] Relativity concerns very large objects whereas quantum theory concerns very small ones. A quantum is the smallest discrete quantity of a physical property, such as electromagnetic radiation or angular momentum. Quantum physics is the study of energy and matter and their complex relationships. Many eminent scientists have been and continue to be excited by quantum theory, particularly because it has opened considerable debate about actual reality, perceived reality, and the blurry area in between.

So what does this have to do with luck? Perhaps it has nothing to do with luck at all—or perhaps it just might. Right or wrong, experts have used quantum theory to explain the blurry area of our perception of reality, where the power of the mind could produce an effect on matter. It is also the area where both ancient and modern philosophies meet science head on.

Who Let the Cat Out?

Some top athletes openly talk about their thoughts on quantum theory as it has benefited their game. Rugby union star Jonny Wilkinson discussed his fight against the fear of not achieving his goals and the breakthrough he had when reading about the quantum thought experiment known as Schrödinger's cat.[21]

Austrian physicist Erwin Schrödinger sought to illustrate quantum theory by imagining a cat sealed in a box with a jar of cyanide and a piece of radioactive material. There is a 50 percent chance, at any given time, that the material has decayed enough to trigger the release of the poison. At that time, quantum physics maintains the cat is both alive and dead; however, as soon as one opens the box and looks inside, one can see the cat is either alive or dead. "It had a huge effect on me," Wilkinson said. "The idea that an observer can change the world just by looking at it, the idea that the mind and reality are somehow interconnected...it hit me like a steam train."

Could this possibly explain how advanced visualization techniques enhance performance? It just might explain how some people seem able to control their lives more skillfully and thereby achieve more success than others. Perhaps quantum physics forms the magical energy behind the law of attraction.

Theoretical physicist Stephen Hawking shares Einstein's belief that a new theory will one day unify the theories of relativity and quantum physics. He calls this a quantum theory of gravity. Unfortunately, such a theory would present an unprecedented challenge. Quantum theory postulates that the act of observing an experiment affects the results. Yet observation is the current cornerstone of scientific inquiry. In *A Briefer History of Time*, Hawking wrote, "Yet if there really were a complete unified theory, it would also presumably determine our actions—so the theory itself would determine the outcome of our search for it.[22]

It does not seem an answer to these questions is likely to surface soon; however, Wilkinson found these ideas helpful, as have others. Einstein believed events that seemingly defy the laws of probability will one day have a scientific explanation. In a 1947 letter to the physicist Max Born, Einstein wrote that he thought he had a continuous-field theory that avoids "spooky action at a distance"[23] and that someone in the future will develop a theory that does not depend on probabilities.

All in Good Time

Now is a good time to delve even more deeply into the esoteric origins of luck, try to find common ground in all of these theories, and bring them back to the real world of poker.

Psychologist Carl Jung viewed luck as "synchronicity"[24] and described it as a meaningful coincidence. So he, too, believed luck is not entirely random. This is very different from Noah Webster's classic-dictionary definition of "luck," which is "a purposeless unpredictable and uncontrollable force that shapes events favorably or unfavorably for an individual, group, or cause."[25]

Jung was so fascinated by synchronicity that he developed his concepts in the 1920s but only published it in 1952, possibly because he knew how controversial it would be. He felt that his paper justified the existence of the paranormal. He held long conversations with Albert Einstein about the possible connection between paranormal synchronicity and the theory of relativity as well as quantum mechanics.

Jung believed his thoughts about synchronicity proved the existence of the collective unconscious—in other words, unrelated events that at first sight appear to be coincidental are, in fact, related because they draw upon the totality of human experience through the ages. This totality includes the whole range of social, emotional, psychological, and spiritual ingredients.

This jibes to some degree with the work of Scottish philosopher and author Sydney Banks, who shared his three principles of mind, consciousness, and thought. Banks believed these three principles explained the entire range of human behavior. However, his philosophy is extremely difficult to understand, let alone employ.

To keep it simple, Banks is attributed with the statement that as many as seventy thousand thoughts each day arise from different parts of our brain. Unfortunately most of them are not helpful. Once we are aware of an unconscious thought, it has reached our conscious mind, and so we can then control what we do with that thought. The options are simple: We can embrace it or banish it because it is only a thought and not a reality. The thoughts that we choose to embrace can then be processed by higher mental powers. This is what Banks describes as "mind."

A further extrapolation of this conclusion leads us to complex questions about a wide range of spiritual and philosophical beliefs. A common and recurring belief is that we can tap into some higher power, and this belief brings much comfort to its supporters. Jung did not believe that life was random either, and he wrote about a similar deeper order leading to spiritual awakening.

You will not find many philosophy books lying open on a poker table, and rightly so. More important to you is the question of how or if you can use these esoteric abstract theories to become a better poker player. So ask yourself this question now: "In a nutshell, if I could draw upon the experience of every great poker player throughout history, what difference would it make to me and my game?"

I know this is a fanciful statement, but I encourage you to at least keep this possibility open. This will be more than enough to stimulate and set free the powerhouse of your unconscious mind. So many champions have chalked up their greatest successes to letting go or getting out of their own way that we would be foolish to take their views lightly.

Not surprisingly, Jung's views have many dissenters who propose alternative conclusions. Their explanations of synchronicity include the failure of our pattern-recognition skills, while others believe synchronicity is no more than highly developed intellectual intuition. For what it is worth, I am most comfortable with this latter explanation because there is so much we can do to improve our intuition. All of the secrets to success that I have described in this book can develop your intuition skills.

I also believe in a collective unconscious, but not necessarily in the same way Jung did. I have access to genetic information that was unavailable to him. I know that human embryos pass through all stages of evolution as they develop. Amazingly, at different times, they display characteristics of fish, reptiles, and birds. In fact, the remnants of fish gills still persist in some people. Occasionally they cause illness but usually are just coincidental discoveries. The brain develops similarly, and its deepest layers, sometimes known as the reptilian brain, are least understood.

If our collective unconscious hides in our brain, my gamble would be that it is inside the amygdala. This is a small but critically important part of our unconscious brain that is home to our emotions and decision-making. Perhaps many of our intuitions are DNA echoes that have been inherited through generations and stored in the amygdala. If so, it is unfortunate that most people's conscious minds are too busy to hear their unconscious minds speak. This is the reason I spend so much time with my clients, teaching them to magnify and ignite their intuition through meditation skills and techniques such as Havening, HeartMath, and hypnosis.

Trust Me, I Am a Nuclear Physicist

It is definitely time for a bit of light relief, so I will conclude this chapter with an interesting little snippet I saw in the *Metro* newspaper in 2010. It concerned two subatomic particles colliding at the speed of light in the Large Hadron Collider, and it quoted Sergio Bertolucci, research director for CERN, the European Organization for Nuclear Research: "'There are known unknowns out there, like dark matter and new dimensions about which we hope to learn,' said Bertolucci. 'But it is possible we will find some unknown unknowns which could be hugely important for mankind.'"[25] I found these comments rather frightening.

My fears increased during 2011, when scientists discovered that neutrinos travel faster than the speed of light—which is impossible if we believe the law of relativity. Worse was to come a few months later when those same scientists checked and found that errors had been caused by flaws in the setup of their equipment. And these are the same people who collide subatomic particles at the speed of light with the possibility of discovering unknown unknowns.

This sounds like the ultimate game of poker. By comparison, you and I are the most sensible people on the planet.

Now, review your notes and thoughts on this chapter. Ask yourself this question: "What three things can I do now that can help me immediately, or at least in the very near future, to make more luck playing poker?" Write your three points below.

The next chapter is the final one, the conclusion of our journey together. I warn my clients as they start their online course or attend my workshops that they are on a journey. It is a journey that will take many unexpected turns and, at times, appear bewilderingly complicated.

However, the final steps are perhaps the easiest, given the dawning realization that there are a lot fewer changes to make in our strategies and processes than we imagined. Indeed, I could summarize it in just one word: *intuition.*

In a Nutshell—Three Nuggets

1.

2.

3.

8

Your Perfect Hand

YOU NOW HAVE the seven secrets in your pocket. Can you remember all of them? Your unconscious mind never forgets anything, so those secrets will be hiding in there somewhere. For now, here is a list to bring them back to the surface:

1. How to achieve your goals
2. Inner confidence
3. Everyone can visualize
4. Mindfulness
5. The three *H*s of Havening, HeartMath, and hypnosis
6. The benefits of logic
7. Mind magic

You have fought through to the final table, and as the dealer flips the seventh card, you are reminded of Moorman's ace on the river. Now it is your turn to shout "Get in!" as you realize everything you have been working on has delivered you your perfect hand. You have ignited your mind skills and, therefore, your game to a level you never knew existed. It is very unlikely that any of the other players can match your commitment. So enjoy the moment, because you deserve it.

What Next?

This book is deliberately not just a list of recommendations designed to make you luckier and more mindful or thereby produce more flow in your life as a poker player. The most important ingredient in your search for greater success will not be the words I have written; it will be your own thoughts that surface, as if from nowhere, and guide you toward what instinctively feels like the right direction.

The focus of my efforts has been to engage with your unconscious mind, plant a few ideas, and put you in touch with the resources that will lead you toward your luck, wherever it hides. Dig up this valuable treasure and use it as you will.

Of course, what works for you may not work for another person and vice versa. But the following statements are historically accurate:

- If you read the whole of this book, then it is *possible* you will find more luck.
- If you also write down key nuggets and your three action points at the end of each chapter, it is *probable* you will find more luck.
- If you also remind yourself daily about your three action points from each chapter, it is *almost certain* you will find more luck.
- If you also tell another person about your three action points from each chapter and how you are going to use them, it is *almost guaranteed* you will find more luck.

Run with the Ball

You may choose to do something else, and it will be very powerful. Many successful business leaders have just one piece of paper on their desk, which they review each morning. This paper is the distilled life essence of their empire; it comprises the few key critical factors that define success or failure. All of these are measurable, and the chief executive officer is happy only when he or she has his or her finger on this pulse.

You will also benefit from a similar approach. Cut and paste all of your chapter nuggets onto one piece of paper. Review this list every morning and pick five items to take action on that day. Review it again at the end of each day and record your score. Even if you did not hit all of your targets, you will still feel happier than you might have expected because you will have exercised a degree of control over your life—and that is something we all want to do more often.

Another suggestion is to use this one page as the front cover of your own book of life. This book would be an informal scrapbook of all the things that are most important to you. The pictures and notes you would include would feature your family and friends, your successes, and your dreams for the future. Your scrapbook would also include all the different ways you will continue to acquire new skills and knowledge and thereby reinvent yourself.

One of the few things I learned during an expensive business-training course was that, just to stand still in today's rapidly changing world, it is necessary to replace 25 percent of your intellectual content each year.

You cannot afford to stand still. The world of poker is ultracompetitive and relentlessly filling with a new breed of young and fearless players.

Every year, allocate part of your budget to self-development, both for you as a person and as a player.

Continue to trust your newly discovered control and appreciation of your unconscious mind. Remember the newborn baby I mentioned in the introduction? It was 99.99 percent complete, lacking only a conscious mind. Years later, it has completed its development. Its conscious mind is now firmly in control and has conveniently forgotten that it still forms only 0.01 percent of its existence.

This conscious mind develops as a result of life experiences and in response to interactions with other people. Some of these experiences will be positive and others far less so. The degree of resultant happiness depends less on the pleasure associated with these experiences than on how this person chooses to think about them.

I sincerely hope you have found at least one idea within this book that will lead you to attract a few more lucky breaks. Perhaps you found many.

Either way, I would like to know. How did it change your life? What value did it hold? Were you surprised by this change, or did you sense that it was waiting for you? What difference did these insights make to your life as a poker player?

I know from discussing luck and related concepts with thousands of clients and delegates that some skills are more easily acquired through sensory channels than through the written word alone. For that reason, I have highlighted important points in italic throughout the book.

These skills form the foundation of my workshop and online coaching courses. Please, feel free to write to me with any comments through my website, drstephensimpson.com. If you have a question, I will do my best to answer that too, either personally or through my blog. Sign up for the blogs and newsletter; they are free and full of tips, insights from other readers, and sometimes free offers. Even better, write a short article, and I'll do my best to publish it.

The more of your five senses you use when developing your mind skills for poker, the better your results will be. This book is a great start, but it is not the end of your journey. I will be adding videos and audiobooks to my website as well as details of upcoming workshops and events. Some of these will be free, so this is another great reason to sign up for my blogs. Remember, the only limits are those you set yourself or that others impose upon you.

Whichever route you take, I wish you a pleasant journey. I hope that the success, health, wealth, and happiness you find at the poker table far exceed your wildest expectations. That said, congratulations on reaching the end of this book. Do you have any questions? E-mail them to me at doc@drstephensimpson.com, and I will reply. Please also post a review of the book so others will know what to expect when they are considering starting this journey with me.

I mentioned in the previous chapter that the greatest gift you can possess as a poker player—and in life, generally—is intuition. This is what the seven secrets will bring you. Who better than Chris Moorman to help me with the final words: "It helps and is extremely important," Moorman says. "Having strong intuition and a lot of experience to aid your decision-making can often give you that extra 10 percent that you need at the very top level of the game. I try to focus on my opponents' mannerisms when they are involved in big pots and guess in my head whether I think they are strong or weak," he explains.

That "guess in my head" is intuition. It is a feeling, and for Moorman, it is in his head. For others it could be a feeling in their guts, their hearts, the hairs on the backs of their necks, or goose bumps.

I wish you many of these feelings. You might even be able to use them against Chris sometime. I look forward to that!

Safe travels.

About the Author

D R. STEPHEN SIMPSON is a world-renowned mind coach, presenter, author, feature writer for *Best You* magazine, and fellow of the Royal Society of Medicine.

As a private mind coach, Dr. Simpson counts many luminaries from the sporting, gaming, entertainment, and business worlds among his clients.

Dr. Simpson has appeared on the BBC, ITV, Sky, Voice of America, and other top international TV and radio programs, as well as in the pages of *Sunday People*, *Glamour*, *Golfing World*, *The Best You Magazine*, *WPT Poker*, and more, sharing his simple, innovative methods for building luck.

As an inspirational speaker, Dr. Simpson has delighted audiences of many thousands in Europe, the Americas, Africa, and Asia.

Additionally, Dr. Simpson works as a mind coach on both the PGA European Tour and the World Poker Tour, helping star performers find their zone, perform in flow, and gain the winning edge.

More details of his work, books, videos, podcasts, and audiobooks can be found on his website, www.drstephensimpson.com.

NOTES

1. "Mind, Body and Soul with Dr. Stephen Simpson," Lee Davy, XLMedia PLC, *PokerUpdate*, December 23, 2014, http://www.pokerupdate.com/ interviews/12232-mind-body-and-soul-with-dr-stephen-simpson/.

2. The Stephen Simpson School of Making Your Own Luck in Poker," Lee Davy, Dr. Stephen Simpson, drstephensimpson.com, December 23, 2014, http://www.drstephensimpson.com/wp-content/uploads/2016/ 09/The-Stephen-Simpson-School-of-Making-Your-Own-Luck-in-Poker-PDF.pdf?a2a87d.

3. Rory Brown, personal communication.

4. Tony Robbins, *Awaken the Giant Within* (London: Simon & Schuster UK, 2012), 303.

5. Abraham Lincoln quote, Albany Law, October 23, 2016, http://www. albanylaw.edu/media/user/celt/albanypptr_stuckey1.pdf

6. Michael Phelps quote, Royal Caledonian Curling Club, October 23, 2016, http://royalcaledoniancurlingclub.org/wp-content/uploads/2011/08/ Mindset-Information-sheet-SIS.pdf

7. Michael Phelps quote, Scottish Swimming, October 23, 2016, https://www.scottishswimming.com/media/1701543/Short-guide-to-Swimmer-Mindset-Mar-16.pdf

8. William Shakespeare quote, Amazon.com. Inc., Goodreads, October 23, 2016, http://www.goodreads.com/quotes/21546-our-doubts-are-traitors-and-make-us-lose-the-good

9. Henry Ford quote, Amazon.com. Inc., Goodreads, October 23, 2016, http://www.goodreads.com/quotes/978-whether-you-think-you-can-or-you-think-you-can-t--you-re

10. Simon Jenkins, *Sports Science Handbook: Volume 2: The Essential Guide to Kinesiology, Sport & Exercise Science* (London: Multi-Science Publishing Co. Ltd., 2005, 80.

11. "Employees, Emotions and Engagement," Mike Ryan, Madison Performance Group, *MADISON*, February 18, 2014, http://www.madisonpg.com/2014/02/employees-emotions-and-engagement.

12. Hans Hofman quote, Amazon.com. Inc., Goodreads, October 23, 2016, http://www.goodreads.com/quotes/70138-the-ability-to-simplify-means-to-eliminate-the-unnecessary-so.

13. Hans Margolius quote, Forbes Media LLC, ForbesQuotes, Thoughts on the Business of Life, October 23, 2016, http://www.forbes.com/quotes/3815/.

14. "Listening for the whispers of truth inside," Sabrina Bolin, Sabrina Bolin, sabrinabolin.com, February 27, 2015, http://www.sabrinabolin.com/listening-for-the-whispers-of-truth-inside.

15. "Harness," abrahamfths, Tangient LLC, Wikispaces, October 23, 2016, http://abrahamfths.wikispaces.com/harness.

16. *Oxford Dictionaries*, s.v. "magic," accessed October 23, 2016, https://www.oxforddictionaries.com.

17. Alexis Carrel Quotes, BookRags Inc., BrainyQuote, October 23, 2016, http://www.brainyquote.com/quotes/quotes/a/alexiscarr158389.html.

18. Robert Graves quote, Wisdom Quotes, October 23, 2016, http://www.wisdomquotes.com/quote/robert-graves.html

19. Paul McKenna, *I Can Change Your Life In 7 Days*, (New York City: Bantam Press, 2010), 196.

20. Stephen Hawking, *A Briefer History of Time* (New York City: Bantam Press, 2008), 15.

21. Will Pavia, "Quantum Physics Puts New Spin on Jonny Wilkinson's Life," *The Times*, September 19, 2008, http://www.thetimes.co.uk/tto/sport/rugbyunion/article2357338.ece.

22. Stephen Hawking, *A Briefer History of Time* (New York City: Bantam Press, 2008), 17.

23. "Einstein's 'Spooky Action at a Distance' Paradox Older Than Thought," *MIT Technology Review*, March 8, 2012, http://www.technologyreview.com/view/427174/einsteins-spooky-action-at-a-distance-paradox-older-than-thought.

24. Carl Jung, *Synchronicity: An Acausal Connecting Principle* (Bollingen, Switzerland: Bollingen Foundation, 1952).

25. Luck definition, Wikipedia, October 23, 2016, https://en.wikipedia.org/wiki/Luck

26. "Large Hadron Collider to Give Answer to Universe's 'Known Unknowns,'" *Metro*, March 30, 2010, http://metro.co.uk/2010/03/30/large-hadron-collider-to-give-answers-to-universes-known-unknowns-203154/.

Made in the USA
San Bernardino, CA
24 July 2020

75708968R00058